Henry Cecil was the pseudony
Leon. He was born in Norwood Green Rectory, near London, England in 1902. He studied at Cambridge where he edited an undergraduate magazine and wrote a Footlights May Week production. Called to the bar in 1923, he served with the British Army during the Second World War. While in the Middle East with his battalion he used to entertain the troops with a serial story each evening. This formed the basis of his first book, *Full Circle*. He was appointed a County Court Judge in 1949 and held that position until 1967. The law and the circumstances which surround it were the source of his many novels, plays, and short stories. His books are works of great comic genius with unpredictable twists of plot which highlight the often absurd workings of the English legal system. He died in 1976.

FATHERS
IN LAW

by

Henry Cecil

HOUSE OF
STRATUS

Copyright © 1965 Henry Cecil

This edition published in 2000 by House of Stratus, an imprint of Stratus Holdings plc, 24c Old Burlington Street, London, W1X 1RL, UK.

www.houseofstratus.com

Typeset, printed and bound by House of Stratus.

A catalogue record for this book is available from the British Library.

ISBN 1-84232-052-1

Contents

CHAPTER ONE

The Night Before

Mary Woodthorpe did not think that she slept at all during the night before she and Hugh were to appear before Judge Bramcote. Of course she had slept part of the time. People who 'haven't slept a wink all night' have probably had, if not enjoyed, at least half their normal sleep. Mary certainly had less than this. Between two and three in the morning she made herself a cup of tea, while Hugh lay sleeping peacefully. She tried to read, but unsuccessfully. She tried more successfully to think the night away. To think of everything that had gone before.

Her wedding, white and happy; even what the vicar said, 'Two things you need for a happy, lasting marriage. You have the one – love. Have you the other – tolerance?' Her honeymoon. Glorious. So glorious that she was even happy when it was over, eager to start this new life together.

And then the happy years, happy for him in everything, for her, too, in the beginning, but later with her happiness sadly qualified, as the months and years went by with never even a hint of a family being on the way. Well, perhaps a hint from time to time, a hint which made things worse because it was always belied.

1

She remembered when a little shyly, a little embarrassed, she first mentioned the matter to her husband. They loved each other dearly, but he had no particular longing for a child. Because he loved her and knew she wanted one, he would have been happy to have one for her sake. But he had to admit that selfishly he realised that, once the family started, he could not receive all Mary's attention. So while, to please Mary, he hoped for children, he bore their absence quite cheerfully.

All the same, when Mary mentioned the matter and wanted to seek help, he agreed to all her suggestions. She remembered this gratefully, because she knew well enough that he did not share her deep and dreadful longing, dreadful because it might never be satisfied.

How many years was it? Three before they went to a doctor. And then another year with temperature charts meticulously kept by her. She didn't mind his teasing her about them, nor his somewhat coarser jibes when her temperature rose above normal. Once it was just flu.

And then more visits to the doctor, and those two days in hospital. This must do it, she had told herself. How she had prayed the night before. And the thought of her prayers then made her pray now for a successful meeting with Judge Bramcote. And then the remembrance that her operation had made no difference made her fearful that Judge Bramcote might have no more effect on her life than the surgeon. She had met plenty of doctors before. But no judges – oh yes, she had. Once. For a few minutes at a party. Mr Justice Richmond. From her point of view a dull, lugubrious man, though the life and soul of the party when intricate legal problems were discussed. But an erudite knowledge of charitable trusts and the doctrine of frustration does not necessarily make for good small talk at a party.

She hoped that Judge Bramcote would be different. Not that she really minded what he was like, so long as he did what she wanted.

And then she thought of those further visits to doctors. And all the unpleasant things that went with them, for her and her husband. She gave him full marks. He certainly showed the tolerance which the vicar had talked about. If she hadn't wanted a child, would she have submitted to all the unpleasantness for her husband's sake? She hoped she would. And then that awful morning when what they did could be described as a clinical performance, not actually under the eye of the doctor but the results of which were to be examined by him microscopically later.

Finally, the worst day of all when they proved that it couldn't be done. He had an obstruction, which could not be removed, and the whole thing was off.

He took her away for a holiday after this, and they discussed adoption. Once again he fell in with her wishes. If she wanted a family, she should have one, even if other people had done all the work. Now there were different sorts of interviews. Not with doctors except once, when their general health was enquired into and pronounced entirely satisfactory. Interviews with professional social workers, people anxious to see whether a child would have a good chance of happiness in such a home. Not an enquiry which can be answered as the result of a couple of visits.

People are on their best behaviour when such enquiries are made. There can never be complete certainty about the prospective adopters unless those who make the enquiries go to live with them for a month or more. You can be on your best behaviour all the time for a weekend perhaps, but not for a month. A number of unsuccessful marriages would never have taken place if the engaged couple had stayed at each other's homes for a month.

But, though it is not practicable for proposed adopters to be visited to this extent, all that could be done was done to see if Mary and her husband would prove satisfactory adopters. Indeed Mrs Lyndhurst, the guardian appointed by the Court to safeguard the child's interests, was a particularly able and imaginative person and took the greatest care in carrying out her investigations.

'The wife,' she wrote in her confidential report to the judge, 'is a charming young woman of 30 who will obviously make a most loving and kindly mother. It may be that she will be too loving and kindly, and the child may be somewhat spoiled. But there is no doubt that the child will enjoy the most loving care. I can only express the hope that he will always enjoy it. That is the only danger in this placement, the possibility that in his early days the child will be too much indulged and that later on he may resent or be irked by the warmth of his adopting mother's affection. As against that, I am personally a firm believer in 1st Corinthians, Chapter 13, and, though I do not claim to speak with the tongue of men or angels, I do believe that love never fails.'

It is not altogether surprising that Mrs Lyndhurst, with her somewhat unusual and individualistic reports, was popular with the judges to whom she reported, and none the less so because she was a particularly attractive woman.

About the husband Mrs Lyndhurst wrote this: 'The husband, aged 31, is a man who will always come second. He has done this literally in most of his activities. He nearly got a rugger blue; he got a blue for cricket, but lost it owing to his not being able to play in the Varsity match; he got a second (a near-first) in his final examinations at

Cambridge, and he will certainly come second to this baby if an adoption order is made. He is a thoroughly nice fellow (I apologise for the word "nice" but I simply cannot find any other to convey what I mean), very fond of his wife, of absolute integrity, and he will be a kind and tolerant father. It is obvious to me that, while he is a willing party to this application, he has no burning desire to be a father, though I do not suggest for a moment that this is the reason that the applicants have so far not had children of their own. He wants this child solely because he knows how desperately his wife wants it. Apart from the unhappiness in which it would involve her, he would not be particularly depressed if an adoption order were refused. I am satisfied, however, that he will take a proper part in bringing up the child, and it may well be that, as the child takes on what from his point of view will be more human form, he may take a real interest in the boy. Especially so, if he turns out to be good at games. In some cases there would be a danger that, as Mr Woodthorpe has been what I might call a successful failure, he would try to drive the boy into succeeding at all the things where he just failed. I do not think this will happen, the keynote of Mr Woodthorpe's character being tolerance. I suspect that this is a home where even fools would be suffered gladly. They would be loved by Mrs Woodthorpe and tolerated by her husband. I recommend that an adoption order be made.'

Mary had never seen this report but she liked Mrs Lyndhurst and had been very much encouraged by her. Over and over again, in the days while she was waiting for the application for adoption to be heard, she had reminded herself of the words which Mrs Lyndhurst had used. She said them again to herself as she sipped her tea that night.

'Of course, it's for the judge, not me, to make the order,' Mrs Lyndhurst had said, 'but I'm quite sure you'll have no difficulty in getting it, no difficulty at all.'

But then she remembered with an icy feeling in her stomach that Mrs Lyndhurst had added: 'No difficulty at all – unless, of course, the mother withdraws her consent. But that's not at all likely.' Not at all likely. That meant it was possible. The mother had signed the consent form apparently willingly enough. But she had the right to withdraw it. Why should she withdraw it? Why shouldn't she?

The fears of a prospective mother-by-adoption are different from but certainly no less than those of an ordinary prospective mother-for-the-first-time. The chances of anything going wrong in England, with an ordinary birth, are small. Each year about one in five thousand mothers dies in childbirth or has a child which dies at birth. More than the number of people killed by lightning (only twelve a year) but still only very few. In all probability everything will be all right.

But, when it comes to adoption, the mother can withdraw her consent at any time up to the making of the order. And, unless she does so capriciously or without thought for the welfare of the child, it will be given back to her. Even though the prospective adopters have had the child for a year or more and will be heartbroken at losing it. It's not like a doll you can replace next day.

But the mother wouldn't withdraw her consent. She mustn't. Why should she put the child out for adoption if she wanted to keep it? Mary knew little about the mother, but the adoption society had told her all it knew. She was an educated girl, who said that she had met a solicitor at a dance, and a baby was the result. She did not even know the solicitor's name, or where he lived. She had no satisfactory means of keeping the child and she thought it would be in his interest to be adopted.

In fact the girl had arrived unannounced at the adoption society's premises with the baby. She spoke of her proposal in such a matter-of-fact way to the representative who interviewed her, that it caused that lady to say quite sharply: 'It's not like leaving a piece of baggage at a cloakroom, you know.'

This had reduced the mother to tears. Eventually the formalities had been gone through, and the baby placed with the Woodthorpes.

What a day that was. Mary remembered it so vividly. At last it had happened. At last. She didn't think then of the problems or pitfalls of adoption law. She had her baby. She had had to wait almost a year. Her joy was as much as a real mother's. And she had the advantage of being up and about at the time. No stitches had to be removed in her case. And she loved it from the start. Just like a real mother. The small thing that was to be hers.

Her husband had looked at it. 'Very nice,' he had said. She knew what he meant, but didn't mind. Now she had them both. Could any happiness be more complete? After the first wonderful month, when the baby most considerately suffered from nothing at all, she realised that happiness could be more complete. The baby wasn't yet hers. But it was. It must be. Another two months and it would be. But at any time within the three months the mother could ask for her piece of baggage back again. Mrs Lyndhurst assured Mary that there was no sign whatever of the mother appearing to have changed her mind. And then came the great day when the mother yet again stated that she wanted the order made.

Mary thought gratefully of the moment when Mrs Lyndhurst gave her that news over the telephone. But later the same day she had been told something which at the time disturbed her. She had been advised by a lawyer friend to have a solicitor to represent them. Both she and her husband asked why this should be necessary in a straightforward case. 'You never know,' their friend had said. 'There are technicalities in these matters, and it's as well to have a lawyer to keep you straight.'

Although she was a little worried at the idea of having to go to a lawyer, she had become most grateful in the end for the advice. They had gone to see a Mr Luttrell, who was recommended to them as having great experience of adoption cases. She remembered his first words.

'Adoption, is it? If I'd got one, you could have that.'

'I beg your pardon?'

'Children are the devil. Horrible to think I was one myself once. And no better than the others. Probably worse. Lucky there are people like you in the world. With girls dropping children all over the place. Wasn't so fifty years ago. People minded then. Nobody cares what you do today. Illegitimate, I suppose?'

'Yes.'

Mary's husband could not resist adding that the father was a solicitor.

'A solicitor, eh? Not in my firm, I hope. What's his name?'

'They don't know.'

'Oh, come, this won't do. Of course they know.'

'They say they don't.'

'Which court is this in?'

They told him.

'This is serious,' he said. 'Tell me all you know about the mother, and her solicitor.'

Mary remembered her sudden fear. Mrs Lyndhurst had said everything would be all right. And now this lawyer was saying it was serious. What was serious? Mr Luttrell told her.

'Now, some judges take the view that the father of a bastard doesn't count. Quite right. He shouldn't. He's had his bit of fun. And that should be that. Now, it's true his consent isn't necessary, but if – and only if – he's liable to contribute to the maintenance of the child either under an agreement or an affiliation order, he is by law entitled to be heard by the Court as to whether an adoption order should be made.'

'Yes, I was told that,' Mary's husband had said, 'but this man didn't even know there was a child. He couldn't have become liable to pay for it. The mother doesn't even know who he is.'

'Quite right,' said Mr Luttrell. 'So the mother says.'

'I don't understand.'

'If what the mother says is true, all well and good. But suppose it isn't?'

'But how can we tell?'

'You can't, without the mother being questioned a good deal more. And probably she is telling the truth. But there are cases where mothers have special reasons for not telling the truth.'

'Why should this be one?'

'Why indeed?'

'Then what is serious?'

'One of the judges at this Court is very difficult about these cases.'

'In what way?'

'He won't just accept the mother's say-so in cases like this.'

'What does he do, then? Refuse the adoption order?'

'Oh gracious, no. He just insists on her being more closely questioned. Sometimes even has her summoned before him so that he can ask the questions. I must admit that he does sometimes get results. Finds people whose addresses he has been assured nobody knows.'

'But how does that hurt us?'

'Well, for one thing, it delays the making of an order; for another it causes everyone a lot of inconvenience; but, worse than anything, while all this is going on, the mother may change her mind and ask for the child back. Indeed, I knew of a case where this happened. The mother was so fed up at being questioned by the judge that she suddenly said she wouldn't answer any more questions and she'd trouble the judge to hand her back the baby.'

'How terrible.'

'Indeed it was, and might have been worse.'

'Worse?'

'Yes – he might have handed it back. Fortunately in that case I was able to satisfy the old fool that the mother was being unreasonable, and so my clients got the child in the end. But it was touch and go.'

'What are we to do, then?'

'You? Nothing. There are two judges at this particular Court. The judge who makes the difficulties is called Hazlewell. I shall now find out whether your application is coming before him.'

'And if it is?'

'Quite simple. I shall try to get the case adjourned to a day when it will come before the other judge, Judge Bramcote.'

'What's he like?'

'A judge after my own heart. A most reasonable man. He doesn't worry about putative fathers – which, by the way, is what gentlemen who behave like your solicitor friend are called.'

'Suppose you can't get the case taken by him?'

10

'I can only try,' said Mr Luttrell, 'but I can try very hard, if necessary.'

Whether or not Mr Luttrell had had to try very hard, he succeeded. The case was to be heard before Judge Bramcote. But, even so, Mary got little sleep. She looked at Hugh still sleeping peacefully in his cot. Tomorrow she would be taking him to court to make him hers. She smiled. And Bill's too, of course, she suddenly thought, and she looked at her husband who was sleeping just as peacefully.

CHAPTER TWO

The Day Before

Bill Woodthorpe had a peaceful night. And he had had a happy peaceful day. In the pavilion at Lords. No one would have thought that he was about to have a baby.

But, though he mostly thought about the cricket or chatted to people around him, he did from time to time think about Hugh. And he was pleased. Mary had no interest in cricket, and this summer for the first time he had been able to go off to Lord's quite happily, knowing that Mary would not even miss him. Hugh had been with them for four months. Four entirely satisfactory months. He was a quiet baby and though, of course, he cried from time to time, he was wonderful at night and seldom a nuisance during the day. And Mary was so happy. Her eyes shone as they used to after they were just married when he came home in the evening. Bill was not particularly imaginative or observant. Indeed, he only realised that Mary's eyes had ceased to shine as much as they used to, when Hugh made them shine again.

He was not in the least jealous. He loved to see Mary happy. In a way she was his child as well as his wife. And to watch her eyes shine with happiness for whatever reason was the greatest pleasure for him. The shining eyes of a woman in love, whether with a man or a baby, are among the sights of the world. To rank with great sunsets. And like sunsets, they are seldom satisfactorily reproduced artificially. A notable exception was provided by Mary Astor at the end of the film of *Dodsworth*.

There was a burst of applause. An impossible catch had been held. A fieldsman had flung himself, as it seemed, about the length of the cricket pitch, and there he lay with the ball safely in his hand well off the ground. He did not venture to throw it up in triumph. Bill's neighbour spoke.

'The finest catch I've seen since Hendren held that one at silly mid-wicket. A half-volley. I forget who the batsman was but he opened his shoulders and drove it straight at him. It was murder. But Hendren held it.'

'Pretty well had to, I suppose,' said Bill, 'in self-defence.'

'You can put it that way. But the crowd stood up for two minutes cheering. Very different from now. Look at that catch. He only got a clap or two.'

'Oh, well,' said Bill, 'it was better than that.'

'You're too young,' said his neighbour, 'you wouldn't remember. I saw Middlesex win the championship in Warner's last year. They were crowds in those days. Look at them now. Hardly enough to fill a charabanc. My boy's quite a cricketer.'

'Really?'

'I can't say I've encouraged him. The game's on the way out. "Take up stock-car racing or whatever it's called," I said. I should have thought there were enough accidents on the road to satisfy people. But not a bit of it. They have to go bashing each other for sport. Or that's what they call it. Who's this fellow coming in? Looks young enough. Bit like my boy.'

Bill continued to chat to his neighbour and eventually mentioned, a little prematurely, that he too had a son. There's nothing like healthy competition.

'Does he bat or bowl?' asked his neighbour, and then after looking at Bill, 'but I suppose he's too young.'

'Eighteen months,' said Bill.

'That is a bit young. But you're a cricketer I should say, to look at you, and, if he takes after you, which'll he do?'

'I bat a bit,' said Bill. 'But he may not take after me. He's not really mine.' The neighbour said nothing but tried to look sympathetic. 'Adopted, you know.'

'Oh, I see. I thought for the moment – I say, that was a nice piece of fielding. I could watch good fielding all day long. But how few there are who make one movement of it. Remember Hobbs and Percy Chapman? But you wouldn't. They didn't pick up the ball and throw it. It went straight from the ground to the wicket in one glorious sweep. What I call poetry. One minute the ball was tearing along the ground towards the boundary and then it was on the way back again before you could breathe out. Adopted, I think you said. Do they show you a lot to choose from or do you have to take what they offer?'

'They just showed us Hugh, and my wife took to him on sight.'

'Fine. Well, it's as good a way as any other. Better, you might say. Nearly lost my wife the second time. And you can't imagine what I went through over the third. Worse than that tie between the West Indies and Australia. But all's well that ends well. I'm a grandfather three times over. Young Sam, the cricketer, was a bit of a mistake. My wife says he was an afterthought. There's a subtle difference, but I still say it was a mistake. But I'm not sorry. He's a good boy. Still, you can't make a mistake with adoption. You can send it back if you don't like it.'

'Before the adoption order's made. Not after.'

'Oh, of course. But you're allowed to have it some time before you make up your mind, presumably.'

'Quite. Three months, as a matter of fact. We make an application to adopt the child, you know, and that's served on the mother. Then the Court appoints the local children's officer, or a probation officer or someone, to go into the whole matter. We have to get the mother's consent in writing, of course. And, until the order's made, she can change her mind and so can we.'

'That's fair enough. I'd have sent our first back if I'd had the chance. Yelled the house down. The second and third weren't so bad, or perhaps I'd got used to the noise.'

'Ours is very quiet.'

'You're lucky. How long ago did you adopt it?'

'Well – as a matter of fact – ' Bill paused for a moment and coloured slightly. 'As a matter of fact the order's being made tomorrow. I'm afraid I was anticipating a bit when I said I had a son.'

'Well, it's just a formality, I suppose.'

'I certainly hope so. My wife would yell blue murder if anything went wrong.'

'You can always get another.'

'You're wrong there. It's not so easy. But even if it were, that wouldn't be the answer. Mary's absolutely devoted to Hugh. She couldn't give him up now. She'd want to kill the girl who took him away. And herself too.'

'Well, I imagine it'll go through all right. You don't strike me as particularly worried.'

'I can't say I am really. Only, for Mary's sake, I wish it were over.'

'What do you have to do? Go before a judge and take the adoption vows or whatever they are?'

'I don't know about any vows. We certainly have to go before a judge.'

'I expect you have to swear something or other. These lawyers are fond of oaths. Don't see much point in them myself the way some people take them. I was on a jury once. Policeman gabbled it off as though it meant nothing. The prisoner was very different. He held the Bible right up and said it very slow and very loud. Odd thing was, the policeman told the truth and the prisoner lied like blazes. So one would have been just as well without it altogether. Better. I'm not a religious man really, but both those chaps were in the wrong. The policeman for treating the Bible like a pack of cards, the prisoner for perjuring his immortal soul.'

'Nobody's told us we'll have to swear anything. And we've been to a solicitor.'

'Well, he should know.'

'We didn't ask him, as a matter of fact.'

'I expect he'd have told you. All the same I don't see why you shouldn't make some sort of promise to bring the child up as if it were your own.'

'But people wouldn't adopt children unless that's what they intended.'

'Same applies to getting married. Most people even today, I suppose, don't get married unless they intend to stay married. Forsaking all others and all that. But they take their vows just the same.'

'Not in a registry office.'

'Don't they make any promises there?'

'I wouldn't know for certain, but I don't think so.'

'Well, you'll soon know in your case. Hope it'll go all right.'

'Thanks. We've had a bit of luck as a matter of fact. We've changed judges.'

'Sounds like changing bowlers.'

'It is a bit. Our solicitor told us that one was technical and made difficulties. So he's got our case before the other.'

'Can you choose them like taxis?'

'Don't ask me. Our solicitor just said he'd change them if he could. And he did. Ours not to reason how.'

The change had in fact been effected quite simply. Mr Luttrell had gone to the Court and issued two applications in other cases in which he was concerned. He had asked for a date when Judge Bramcote was sitting. There was no difficulty in obtaining this. He then went before Judge Hazlewell.

'Your Honour,' he said, 'I have two applications before Judge Bramcote on the 13th. I also have an adoption matter before your Honour on the 12th. It would be a great convenience if all these cases could be heard on the same day. I wonder if your Honour would be prepared to adjourn the adoption case to Judge Bramcote's list.'

'Will it take long?' asked the judge.

'No, your Honour,' said Mr Luttrell and added incautiously, 'only a few minutes.'

'Only a few minutes for an adoption case?' queried the judge somewhat severely. 'You seem to treat it like the sale of a motorcar. Will it be on hire purchase by any chance?'

Mr Luttrell forced a smile.

'Forgive me, your Honour. Your Honour is perfectly right to reprove me. What I should have said is that there is no opposition from the mother and the guardian has made a favourable report.'

'And what about the father? Does he consent too?'

'He's a putative father, your Honour, and his consent is not necessary.'

'Has he been served?'

'He has never contributed to the maintenance of the infant, your Honour.'

'Has he been served, Mr Luttrell?'

'He's not entitled to be served, your Honour.'

'I wish you could answer a direct question directly, Mr Luttrell. Has he been served?'

'No, your Honour. We don't even know where he is.'

'Have you tried to find out?'

'The mother says it was a casual acquaintance.'

'A lot of them say that to cover someone else.'

'We have no reason to believe this is the case here, your Honour.'

'What steps – ' began the judge, and then stopped. 'What it really comes to is that you'd prefer Judge Bramcote to deal with the matter.'

'I have two other applications before the learned judge,' said Mr Luttrell.

'I would have been more favourably impressed with your application, Mr Luttrell,' said the judge, 'if you'd just said you want my learned brother to hear this case. I should certainly have acceded to such an application. Personally I think it would be an excellent thing if, where possible, people were allowed to choose their judges. What better tribunal can parties have than the one they ask for? Of course, if they can't agree on a judge, that's another matter. But in your case there's no opposition to the application, so you shall certainly have Judge Bramcote to deal with it. I only wish you'd left out the trimmings.'

'It's very difficult for advocates,' said Mr Luttrell. 'The late Mr Justice Swift said that one should wrap things up.'

'No doubt that's how he liked it. I should have thought that by now, Mr Luttrell, you would have known that I don't. But you shall still have Judge Bramcote. But just one word of warning to you. One day an unknown, unserved putative father may make trouble.'

'I'm much obliged to your Honour,' Mr Luttrell said, and was more than ever thankful from his clients' point of view that his application had been granted.

Bill and Mary knew none of the details. They were quickly given the good news that the warm-hearted, non-technical Judge Bramcote was to hear the case.

'They say the judge we've got is a very nice fellow. I'm quite looking forward to it as a matter of fact. Never been in Court before. Of course this isn't actually in Court. Adoption cases are always heard privately in the judge's room.'

There was a loud appeal for lbw. It was rejected.

'I've done a bit of umpiring,' said Bill's neighbour. 'Bit like judging, I suppose. The barrister who shouts loudest doesn't necessarily win, I imagine, any more than at cricket. But it's rather terrifying in small matches. I mean, if the colonel's bowling and you're dining with him afterwards, and he gives a loud appeal.'

'That depends on the colonel, I should imagine,' said Bill.

'You're dead right. Nine out of ten people forget a bad decision – or one they think's bad, but with the tenth one it rankles. And then there's an atmosphere afterwards. There are bound to be wrong decisions. The thing's too critical sometimes. Not as many as at tennis, though. I hope you won't have one tomorrow.'

'Thanks,' said Bill. 'As far as I can see, the whole thing's cut and dried, but I'll be glad when it's over for my wife's sake.'

'What'll you do to celebrate? Take her out somewhere?'

'Out? With Hugh at home? Our going out days are over for the moment.'

'Baby-sitters?'

'Don't you believe it,' said Bill. "I dare say that in time we'll get round to it. But for the moment she'll be the only baby-sitter in our house in the normal way. I suppose she may put me on when it's absolutely necessary. But she won't trust anyone else with Hugh at present.'

Bill had a pleasant day at Lord's. Cricket is a friendly game and neighbours talk to each other easily. Bill was glad to have been able to talk about Hugh to someone. He wasn't really worried. It was bound to be all right, but if it wasn't, the result didn't bear thinking of. So occasionally, just for a moment, when he pictured Mary's desperate grief at losing Hugh, he had a panic. But then someone made a really good stroke, and he felt better.

CHAPTER THREE

The Day

'Sleep well, darling?' Mary asked Bill the next morning.

'Wonderful. And you?'

She did not answer and he did not ask her again.

'What shall I wear?' she asked. 'The green with the straw hat?'

'That would be fine.'

'Or the blue, do you think? With the same hat.'

'You look lovely in that.'

'Then you prefer it to the green?'

'I wouldn't say I preferred it.'

'You mean you like the blue better?'

'I think they're both nice.'

'Nice? You mean you don't like either. What about my new suit? Or will it be too hot?'

'It might be a little warm.'

'But I won't want a coat.'

'There is that.'

'Do you really like the suit? You've never said much about it.'

'It's charming.'

'Not just nice.'

'Very nice.'

'Would you like it better than the green or the blue?'

'Not better. As well.'

'Then you don't like any of them.'

'Of course I like them.'

'But you distinctly said you didn't.'

'I didn't, really.'

'You said they were nice, didn't you? Do you know a worse word to throw at a girl?'

'I meant it nicely. Oh dear, there I am again. No, really, darling, I love all your dresses.'

'No discrimination.'

'None at all,' he said firmly, 'when you're in them. I only see you. I don't notice the clothes.'

'Other people do. You wouldn't like me not to look nice, would you?'

'Nice?' he queried.

They both laughed.

'I shall wear black,' she said, 'with a white hat. That'll fetch him.'

'Wonderful idea.'

'Or white with a black hat?'

'Either.'

'Which?'

'Well,' he said eventually, 'on the whole black with a white hat.'

'Then you think I'm too fat to wear white?'

'I never even hinted at it.'

'Then why did you say black with white?'

'I meant to say one or the other.'

'Then you just said anything. You tossed up for it. That's not much help to me.'

'You know perfectly well,' said Bill, 'that whatever I say, you'll wear what you decide.'

'You may be surprised to know that I take a lot of notice of what you say.'

'Not about your clothes.'

'Perhaps you're right. Anyway, tell me how I look.'

She tried first one and then another, and then a third and fourth and back to the first again. At this stage Bill suggested that they might have breakfast first or they'd be late. The word 'late' had an electrifying effect on Mary. She put on a black frock and got out a white hat.

'That's settled,' she said.

But later, when Judge Bramcote actually saw her, she was in green.

They arrived early at the Court and had to wait an agonising quarter of an hour before Mrs Lyndhurst arrived. But there was still no Mr Luttrell.

'How are you?' said Mrs Lyndhurst warmly. 'Sleep well?'

'So-so,' said Mary.

'That's better than most of them,' said Mrs Lyndhurst. 'If it were my turn I wouldn't sleep at all. You slept like a top, I expect, Mr Woodthorpe.'

'Splendid, thank you.'

'They always do,' said Mrs Lyndhurst. 'Just the reverse of the other thing. I slept beautifully the night before my first baby, but my husband was a wreck. With adoptions it's the other way round. Well, I'm glad you've nothing to worry about. Lucky we've got Judge Bramcote.'

'I'm so relieved,' said Mary.

'And well you might be,' said Mrs Lyndhurst. 'Judge Hazlewell's a good enough judge in his own way. But he's so pernickety. Ten to one he'd have adjourned this case for at least a month.'

'I couldn't have borne it,' said Mary.

'Well, you'd have had to,' said Mrs Lyndhurst, 'like the others. Ah, here's the man who's saved you from that dreadful fate.'

23

Mr Luttrell had arrived. He shook hands with all of them. 'I'm afraid I've a slight disappointment for you,' he began, and then, as he saw Mary's colour change, hastily said: 'Oh – it's nothing to worry about. But I'm afraid the judge can't take your case first. He's in the middle of trying a case where one of the barristers has to get away to the High Court. And he's promised to finish it before he does yours. That's all. I don't suppose he'll be very long.'

Mary was so relieved that it was nothing worse, that her disappointment at having to wait was much less than it would otherwise have been.

'Give you a chance to see the old boy in court first,' went on Mr Luttrell. 'It's all experience. You may want to send your boy to the Bar. Funny if you did. Or a solicitor even. We're the lower branch, you know. Very humble. But between you and me I don't know what we've got to be humble about. Our exams are harder and cover much wider ground. We usually spend five years in getting qualified, while a barrister spends only three. And, more important than that, we know something about the job before we're qualified, while a barrister knows almost nothing. He learns most of it afterwards. But the law's a funny thing.'

They went into court and after a short time Judge Bramcote came in.

'Be uncovered in court,' said the elderly usher as everyone stood up. No one took his hat off for the very good reason that he'd have been told pretty smartly to take it off if he had come into court with it on, even if the judge wasn't sitting. The judge bowed to counsel and sat down. Everyone else followed suit.

'Clarke against Evans, part heard,' said the clerk, and the judge closed his eyes.

Judge Bramcote had at one time had a slight affection of the eyelids which made it more comfortable for him sometimes to keep his eyes closed. He remained fully awake but it was a little disconcerting for witnesses or advocates who were not aware of his habit. Once a boy of seventeen was in the witness box and he suddenly noticed that the judge was apparently asleep. It so happened that the witness box was very close to the advocate who was questioning him.

'Where were you at ten-thirty on the night of the thirty-first of October?' he was asked.

'Having a bit of shut-eye,' said the boy, and then very boldly added in a stage whisper, 'like him.'

A stage whisper is intended to be heard, but the boy had certainly not intended the judge to hear it.

'What did you say?' said the judge, apparently still asleep.

The boy was dumb.

'I didn't get the last part of that answer,' repeated the judge. 'The witness dropped his voice.'

He opened his eyes and looked at the boy.

'I quite understand,' he said, 'that you find it difficult to give evidence. I don't suppose you've been in Court before and you probably feel nervous. We all understand that. But you must try to speak up. Otherwise I shall be continually asking you to do so and that will make you more nervous than ever. Now, I've got down: "At ten-thirty I was having a bit of shut-eye." What did you say after that?'

This was the first time this boy had ever taken an oath and he knew that to tell lies in the witness box was a serious matter. If you were found out, that is. And he knew that several people at least must have heard what he said.

He looked round despairingly for help. The judge noticed his apparent terror.

'I know you feel nervous,' he said in kindly tones, 'but there's no need to upset yourself unduly. No one is going to be unkind to you or shout at you or anything like that. That sort of thing is reserved for the films – and possibly other countries. No one bullies witnesses in this country, certainly not in this court. Now come along, just repeat what you said after' – the judge looked down at his notebook – 'after "shut-eye".'

The boy gulped.

'Like him,' he whispered.

'Like him,' repeated the judge and wrote it down. 'And who was "him"?' he asked, and added: 'but do please keep your voice up. I only just heard what you said. Try to speak as loud as I do. Say "like him".'

Again the boy whispered it.

'Come, you must do better than that,' said the judge. 'You said the first part quite well. What was it?'

He looked at his note again and repeated. 'At ten-thirty I was having a bit of shut-eye. Now you say that, and add "like him" at the end.'

Almost in despair the boy said loudly: 'At ten-thirty I was having a bit of shut-eye like – ' and then his voice failed and the 'him' was in a whisper.

'That's much better,' said the judge, 'except for the last word. Now let's get on. What was I asking you? I've forgotten.'

Normally counsel would have prompted the judge, but for once no one did.

'Mr Lancaster, can you help me? What was I asking the witness?'

'I'm afraid I've forgotten too,' said counsel, telling a lie which would have brought him no rebuke from the Benchers of his Inn.

'Oh, well,' said the judge, 'if it was important I'll remember it later,' and the incident closed. But from that time Judge Bramcote was familiarly known as 'Old Shut-eye'.

Mary had been told of his nickname, but not of the story which gave rise to it.

'When the Court rose,' said counsel, 'I had just completed my submission on the issue of estoppel. I now come to Central Property and High Trees.'

The judge opened his eyes, which he still closed sometimes from habit.

'Are you going to rely on High Trees?' he asked.

'Yes, your Honour.'

'What time do you want to be in the High Court?'

'Immediately after lunch, your Honour.'

'Well, if you're really relying on High Trees, you won't get there. A full argument on that subject will take, I should think – ' the judge paused, and thought for a moment. 'It will take,' he went on, 'about four days.'

Counsel looked at each other, and the judge closed his eyes.

'Well, what do you want to do about it?' he asked.

There was a whispered conversation between counsel. Then one of them spoke.

'Perhaps, if your Honour would give us a few minutes, we will be able to resolve the difficulty.'

'Certainly,' said the judge. 'I've an adoption case to hear and I'll take it now while you discuss the matter.'

The judge rose and went to his room.

'That's the third time I've seen that happen,' said Mr Luttrell. 'You're in luck. There's a lot of controversy about this case of High Trees. Whenever anyone raises it here, the judge says it'll take four days to argue and off they go and settle the case.'

'But why?' asked Bill.

'Why? Expense,' replied Mr Luttrell. 'Four days here, eight in the Court of Appeal and a dozen in the House of Lords. And all over six and eightpence.'

'Six and eightpence!' said Bill incredulously.

'Not literally,' said Mr Luttrell. 'But, when you think of what the cost of all these hearings is going to be, it'll have to be a pretty large sum in dispute to make it worth while. A couple of hundred pounds would be made to look pretty silly.'

'Well, I'm very grateful to those trees,' said Mary. 'May they grow higher and higher.'

A few minutes later they were shown into the judge's room. He still had his gown on but had removed his wig. He greeted them most affably and glanced admiringly first at Mrs Lyndhurst and then at Mary.

'Come along in and sit down. I'm glad to say your case isn't going to take four days.'

'I'm glad to hear that, too, your Honour,' said Mary.

'I bet you are,' said the judge. 'Don't suppose you slept much last night.'

'I didn't sleep a wink as a matter of fact,' said Mary, starting to love this judge – not, of course, as much as Hugh and Bill but momentarily very much indeed.

'Well, I'm pleased to say,' went on the judge, 'that there are no complications in your case. All the hard work's been done already,' and he again looked admiringly at Mrs Lyndhurst.

'Some people think that adoption's little more than a formality. But it isn't, you know. It's very serious. But, as I said, by the time a case gets to me all the work's been done. I know all about your previous convictions and that sort of thing.'

He smiled.

'I'm quite sure that the child couldn't go to a better home. I know Mrs Lyndhurst agrees, because she's already said so. Not changed your mind, Mrs Lyndhurst?'

'No indeed, your Honour.'

'And I suppose you haven't either?' asked the judge, looking first at Mary and then at Bill. 'Just as well to know before we tie the little fellow up for life. Good little chap. I saw him in Court. Not a word. Some of them scream the house down.'

'No, we haven't changed our minds,' said Mary, and her eyes shone like Mary Astor's.

'Well, that's good,' said the judge. 'For I'm sure the young man would have been most disappointed. What's he going to be, I wonder. His father's a solicitor, I gather. I hope he takes more care with his clients. You're an accountant, Mr Woodthorpe,' he went on. 'Well, you can't go wrong in that profession these days. You govern the world pretty well. And I'm glad to see you're a cricketer. I don't suppose Mrs Woodthorpe's much interested.'

'No, your Honour.'

'My wife isn't either. But that won't worry either of you now. The boy's name is Hugh. D'you want to keep Hugh? Or to add any other names?'

'We'd just like Hugh, your Honour.'

'Well, one name's enough for anyone, unless your surname is Smith or Jones or something. Then you need half a dozen. The child's not been christened yet, I gather. Have you made arrangements with the vicar?'

'Yes, your Honour,' said Mary, 'but we wanted to wait till he was really ours.'

'I know,' said the judge. 'Most people do. But, if you honestly believe in baptism, surely it should be done as soon as possible?'

'But godparents, your Honour?' queried Bill. And Mary could have hit him. Why put a spoke in the wheel at this stage? It was all going so beautifully. But she need not have worried.

'Yes, there is that,' said the judge. 'If for some reason an adoption order were refused and the child went back to the mother, and you'd got Uncle Arthur and a couple of friends as godparents it might be rather awkward. How could they discharge their duties as godparents? So perhaps you're right. Now, Mrs Lyndhurst, is there anything you want to add to your report?'

'No, thank you, your Honour.'

'Good,' said the judge. 'Well, I shall make the order with very much pleasure, and I hope you will all be very happy. But I also hope the young man isn't as good as this all his life. It wouldn't be natural.'

The judge stood up and shook hands with Mary and Bill and they went out, Mary's eyes shining with a wholesome mixture of love and tears. Suddenly they heard a voice.

'Remember me?' said Mr Luttrell. He had done nothing before the judge except bow and smile, but he had earned his fee when he arranged for Judge Bramcote to hear the case.

'I'm so sorry,' said Mary and Bill together. 'We can't thank you enough,' went on Mary. 'What a wonderful judge. I can't tell you how happy you've made us.'

'Fine,' said Mr Luttrell. 'It wouldn't have been like that before Judge Hazlewell.'

Mr Luttrell was right. It would not have been the same before Judge Hazlewell. And, had he tried the case, the history of Mary and Bill might have been very different.

CHAPTER FOUR

Godfathers

'Hath this child been already baptized or no?' asked the vicar. There was no reply. This is quite normal. Presumably the reason why the question is seldom answered is because the parents leave it to the godparents and vice versa. Of course in the ordinary case the only people who can know are the parents. A godparent could only truthfully answer 'not as far as I know', or 'to the best of my knowledge and belief, no.' Answers which would take most vicars a little by surprise. But usually no one says anything and for once silence is treated as a negative answer. Sometimes the vicar himself says 'No?'

When Hugh was christened, no one could truthfully have answered the question, but this was not the reason for no one answering. The vicar said 'No?' and proceeded with the service. In fact the vicar was right. Hugh had been known as Hugh but not christened. After the service was over the vicar invited Mary and Bill and the godparents to the vicarage for a glass of sherry. He was a new vicar and this certainly made a good impression on all concerned.

The godparents chosen by Mary and Bill had been a rich adopted uncle called Sir Nicholas Bent, a friend of Bill's who was a slow bowler, and one of Mary's closest girlfriends.

The vicar handed round the sherry and allowed a certain amount of small talk before he disclosed the real reason for his invitation.

'A very good baby,' he said. 'I don't suppose you remember whether you were, Sir Nicholas?'

'I can't say that I do. But I once saw a man who said he had even earlier recollections.'

They were incredulous and asked for details.

'I was in India at the time,' said Sir Nicholas, 'and happened to wander into the High Court in Bombay. A young man was in the witness box. His actual age was of paramount importance in the case. I suppose he was alleging infancy or something of the sort. "When were you born?" asked counsel. "On the 20th November 1914," said the young man. "But you can't know that yourself," said the judge. "You only know what you've been told." "I know I was born on the 20th November 1914," persisted the young man. "You actually remember being born, do you?" asked counsel. "Certainly." "Did it hurt?" asked the judge. "Not particularly," replied the young man. I enjoyed that "not particularly",' said Sir Nicholas.

'Well, I can't cap that,' said the vicar, 'but I certainly remember being christened.'

'Not really?'

'Yes, really. It was only ten years ago. I'm a comparative latecomer in the Church. That's why I've asked you to come and have a chat after the service. I hope you don't mind. Another glass of sherry?'

'No, thank you, vicar,' said Sir Nicholas, and they all followed suit.

'Now, please sit down,' said the vicar. 'The trouble with converts,' he went on, 'is that they're too enthusiastic. I'm afraid I'm a good example.'

'From what were you converted, may I ask?' said Sir Nicholas. 'Not Buddhism, by any chance?'

'No indeed. From nothing. That was a great advantage. I had nothing to unlearn. No prejudices, no beliefs. A clean slate. Wonderful start. Same as this baby. That's where you come in, Sir Nicholas, and the other godparents. It's a heavy responsibility.'

Sir Nicholas Bent, aged 64, chairman of his local justices, one-time MP, retired from the army with the rank of brigadier, was beginning to regret taking on the job. He was not going to be cross-examined by a 35-year-old vicar, even if he was an enthusiastic converted Christian.

'I'm afraid I shan't be able to stay very long,' he began.

'I won't keep you any longer than I have to,' said the vicar, 'but I feel sure that a man of your age and, may I say, distinction, will be only too pleased to hear what I expect from my godparents.'

'Your godparents?'

'Godparents of children I christen. I feel a similar responsibility towards you as that which you should feel towards the child. Are you sure you won't have that glass of sherry?'

Sir Nicholas took a swift look round at his friends. This time he gave the signal to accept.

'Cheers,' said the vicar. 'Now, first of all,' he went on, 'a few words about the devil and all his works. Sir Nicholas, as by far the oldest of you, must know more about them than the lot of us put together.'

'I am not yet in my dotage,' said Sir Nicholas, who was irked by this repeated reference to his age. In fact he was sensitive on the subject and did not give his birthday in *Who's Who*.

'You're not a year more than 67,' said the vicar. 'I'll warrant that.'

'You're quite right,' said Sir Nicholas. 'I'm 64.'

'I don't suppose you'll look much older than you do already when you're 67. Even when you're 70,' he added.

'You mean I look 70, do you?' asked Sir Nicholas, with some asperity.

'A young and healthy 70,' said the vicar. 'As a matter of fact I thought that was your age. I said 67 because I always knock off two or three years to please people. That's one of the permissible lies. At least I think so. Now for the devil and all his works. Have you had great difficulty in resisting him, Sir Nicholas? Indeed, have you resisted him at all?'

Sir Nicholas remained fiercely silent.

'Come along, Sir Nicholas. We're all friends, and Hugh won't be able to take it in yet. Unless he's like your Indian witness.'

'Vicar,' said Sir Nicholas, 'I have lived the normal life of a respectable man and I don't propose to be cross-examined about it.'

'The sin of pride,' said the vicar, 'is not by any means the worst, I assure you, but I hope you will do your best to see that this child does not suffer from it. Too often I find that godparents think their duties are limited to taking part in the baptism service and remembering a few birthdays and Christmases. That isn't it at all, you know. The religious instruction of this child is committed to your care, no doubt in concert with the parents, but it is still primarily your responsibility.'

'What a lovely word "parents",' said Mary. Then she added: 'I'm sure Uncle Nicholas will make a wonderful godfather, vicar.'

'There's no need to put in a plea for me, Mary,' said Sir Nicholas. 'I'm quite capable of defending myself.'

'Defending?' said the vicar. 'No one's attacking you, I assure you, Sir Nicholas; it is only because you are the oldest. Everything I have said applies equally to the other godparents.'

'That they'll look the same as they do now when they're 70?' asked Sir Nicholas.

The vicar laughed.

'You do worry about your age, don't you, Sir Nicholas,' he said. 'I can't think why. There are lots of people older than you. You're still in the coronary thrombosis bracket, I may tell you. No one's old till he's past that point, whatever age he may look.'

Sir Nicholas got up.

'I'm afraid I must be going,' he said. 'Thanks for the sherry, and the sermon.'

'I'd just like to add a word or two,' said the vicar. 'You may say – quite rightly – that the child is at present too young to understand any religious instruction, and will be for some years. True enough. But, unless you regularly see this child up till the age when he can begin to understand elementary teaching, what chance have you of teaching him anything? You must have his confidence before he'll learn anything from you. And he can't have confidence in you unless constantly in your company. So please grow up with this child until he is old enough to make decisions of his own. You will be well rewarded, I can promise you. The trust of an animal is a wonderful thing in life to have. The trust of a child is immeasurably greater. Please see that you all attain it. Then and then only will you be able to carry out the promises you made not an hour ago. So sorry you all have to go.'

They said goodbye and walked away in silence. Nothing could spoil Mary's happiness. Even the possibility that Sir Nicholas would never speak to any of them again. They could all feel the thunderclouds, and wondered when the storm would break. Sir Nicholas strode on in silence. But eventually he spoke.

'Hell and damnation,' he said. 'Hell and damnation,' he repeated, 'the fellow's right.'

CHAPTER FIVE

Call from a Stranger

Hugh was just over eighteen months old when the adoption order was made. From that moment Mary's happiness was as complete as human happiness can be. She never ceased to be thankful for it. It never grew stale. She never took it for granted. Her child and her husband. She had them both. She wished that everyone could be as happy and, kind and generous as she had been before Hugh became hers, afterwards she tried even harder to help the less fortunate.

It was a wonderful life. Bill loved to see Mary so happy and, as Mrs Lyndhurst had anticipated, began to take a far greater interest in Hugh as he started to look and behave more like a real person, and even to talk. Once Bill even missed a cricket match to be with the boy.

One day, when Hugh was about two and a half, he was playing in the front garden when a stranger stopped to look at him.

'Hello, young man,' said the stranger, but Hugh regarded him coldly, as children often do when someone out of their world tries to draw them into conversation. The stranger was not offended.

'Having a good time?' he asked.

Hugh did not answer. Then Mary came out.

'Lovely boy you've got there,' said the stranger.

'Thank you,' said Mary, 'we think so.'

'Looks just like you,' said the stranger. 'The spitting image. Pity he's not a girl.'

'D'you really think he's like me?' asked Mary.

'No doubt at all.'

'Well, that's odd,' said Mary. 'He's adopted.'

'You don't say,' said the stranger. 'No kidding?'

'It's a fact,' said Mary.

'Well, it's an astonishing coincidence. I'd have sworn you were his mother. But I suppose a child grows to look a bit like the person who brings him up. Like husbands and wives grow to look like each other in a way. They use the same expressions and look the same when they use them.'

'I expect that's it,' said Mary.

'He's a fine boy, anyway,' said the stranger. 'Aren't you frightened to leave him by himself in the front garden? Someone might run away with him.'

'Nonsense,' said Mary, 'that doesn't happen in England.'

'Not often, I agree. But it does happen. And little boys are quite valuable, you know. But he's a bit too old. For one thing he can talk. No, on second thoughts, I think you're right.'

'I'm glad to hear it,' said Mary. 'I think I'd go mad or something if I lost Hugh.'

'Hugh, is it? A good name. They nearly called me Hugh as a matter of fact. Well, I mustn't keep you. Good morning.'

'Good morning,' said Mary, and the stranger walked on.

A few days later he came again. He waited till Mary came out.

'Good morning,' he said. 'I was here the other morning.'

'I remember,' said Mary. 'You were frightened at first that Hugh might be kidnapped.'

'Yes. Silly of me. He's much too old. Adopted, I think you said. Forgive my asking, but how long did it take before you felt he was really yours? Or do you never feel for it as you would for your own child? I'm afraid I'm being very impertinent.'

'Not at all,' said Mary. 'Hugh's been mine from the very first moment.'

'Wonderful,' said the stranger. 'I wonder why his mother gave him up.'

'Couldn't give him a proper home, I think,' said Mary.

'What about the father?'

'Hasn't got one.'

'Well, he must have one somewhere.'

'I suppose so. But no one knows who he was. Just a casual acquaintance.'

'I see. I'm afraid you must think it very odd of me to ask all these questions. As a matter of fact I'm interested in adoption. Met a man once who ... but I mustn't keep you. Goodbye.'

And he walked away.

The stranger repeated his visits until it became quite a normal thing for him to stop and chat to Mary over her front gate. After he'd been calling for a fortnight he said: 'D'you remember I once said I'd met a man?'

'Met a man?' asked Mary, not understanding.

'Just as I was going off one morning. I said I'd met a man who ... and then I didn't finish the sentence.'

'No,' said Mary, 'I don't remember.'

The incident had made no impression on her.

'I told you I was interested in adoption.'

'Yes, I remember you saying that.'

'And then I started to tell you about a man but I didn't finish the sentence and went off.'

'That's why I don't remember, I expect,' said Mary. 'But why are you telling me all this?'

'Only that the man is this boy's father. Forgive me, I must get on.'

CHAPTER SIX

More about the Stranger

Mary was terror-stricken. She rang Bill at his office at once. He dropped everything and came home.

'What can it mean?' she asked desperately. 'Is it a warning, or a threat, or what?'

'There's nothing anyone can do,' said Bill. 'He's legally ours and no one can take him away from us. That's certain.'

'What about kidnapping?' said Mary. 'He mentioned that the second time I saw him. I thought he was just being silly. But now it makes some horrible kind of sense.'

'But, if anyone were going to kidnap the child, they wouldn't come and say so first.'

'That's true, of course. But then what does the man mean? Or want?'

'Could be just a busybody. P'raps he likes hurting people, or frightening them.'

'But why did he come to us? How did he know Hugh was adopted? Ah – I remember. He pretended that he thought Hugh was just like me. I can see now. He did that to make me say he was adopted. We've never pretended anything else, so I told him.'

'Well, there's only one thing to do,' said Bill. 'I'll speak to the fellow myself. I'll soon find out what he's after.'

'I'm so frightened.'

'Now that's one thing you needn't be. I tell you, nothing – no one can take Hugh away from us.'

'I love to hear you say it – but what is he after?'

'I'll find that out. What time does he usually come?'

'It varies. Sometimes between half-past ten and twelve.'

'Right. The office'll have to take care of itself.'

The next day Bill waited at home, but not in the garden. They decided that he would not show himself until the man had stopped to talk to Mary. Bill stayed at home all day but the man never came. The same happened the next day.

'I can't stay at home for ever,' he said after that. 'You give me a ring when he comes. Try to keep him in conversation and I'll nip back in a cab.'

'It'll take you over half-an-hour. How'll I keep him that long?'

'All right. I'll stay tomorrow.'

But tomorrow produced no stranger. So Bill went back to the office. Two days later the man appeared. Mary's heart jumped when she saw him. He looked over the gate, saw her terrified face, raised his hat, smiled and walked on. She rushed to the gate after him, and then stopped. What could she say? If only Bill were there. As if he had heard her, the man turned round when he was twenty yards ahead, raised his hat again, smiled, turned again and went on.

Mary rushed into the house again and telephoned Bill. He tried to comfort her, but comfort for her needed more than words.

'I tell you what,' he said, 'we'll go straight round and see Mr Luttrell. I'll ring from the office to see if he's available, and I'll say it's urgent. But I'm sure there's nothing to be afraid of. Hugh is ours. Ours for always. Really.'

This was a help to Mary. Something was going to be done. They were going to see a lawyer, and not merely a lawyer but the one who knew all about the case. After all, he had appeared for them before the judge. It's true that he had had to say nothing, but he was partly responsible for the order being made. He would see that Hugh remained theirs. Remained theirs? What a terrible thought even to imagine anything else. Suppose the man were the father himself? What could he do about it?

She waited for Bill's telephone call to confirm. She prayed that Mr Luttrell would see them at once. While she waited, she comforted herself with remembering what Bill had said. Hugh is ours. Nothing can take him away. And then she terrified herself by imagining that they lost him. At last the telephone rang. It was all right. She could go straight round to Mr Luttrell and Bill would meet her there. She didn't even change her clothes. It required an emergency of this kind to prevent her. All the same, as she hurried along to Mr Luttrell's office, she felt sure that she was improperly dressed to appear before a solicitor. The fact that she did not even hesitate about the matter showed how desperate she was, as Mary was a woman who would almost have changed if there were a fire and she were not properly dressed for the neighbours to see.

She met Bill at the solicitor's office and he saw them at once. 'Now, what's all this?' he said, after shaking hands and getting them seated. 'Have you changed your minds and want to hand the little fellow back? That can't be done, I'm afraid. But don't be upset. You can always put him out for adoption.'

They hastily explained what had happened.

'I see,' he said. 'How very odd. I wonder what it's all about. But don't distress yourselves. Nothing untoward can happen. The adoption order was properly made. The mother consented. She acknowledged receipt of the notice of the hearing and said that she did not oppose the making of an order and did not want to appear on the hearing. The father, whoever he is, had no right to be heard and his consent wasn't necessary.'

'Then what is this man doing? What does he want? Who is he?'

'It's certainly strange,' said Mr Luttrell. 'It can't be just a coincidence that he's called on you. The chances against that are millions, if not billions to one.'

'I don't quite understand.'

'It's quite simple. Your case was conducted under a serial number. That is to say, although your name and address and everything about you was disclosed to the Court, the documents served on the mother contained only a number. So she couldn't tell who you were or where you lived. The father never had any documents served on him at all. So he would know nothing at all. All the mother would know is the Court which was asked to make the order. Now, it is quite true that coincidences do happen in life, but in my opinion it is absolutely impossible that by pure coincidence the father or someone who knew him happened to look over your garden fence. The man who called on you must have either known for certain that Hugh was your adopted child or he must have had information very near to that; for example, that you lived in that particular road or something of the sort.'

'But how could anyone find out?' asked Bill.

'That is certainly a question. But there, you do get odd coincidences. One person gets talking to another and the information that you have an adopted child which once belonged to a woman called ... called ... well, of course, I don't remember the name – called, well, whatever her name was – goes all over the place, and it is certainly not beyond the bounds of possibility that the information reached by chance someone who knew the father. It isn't at all likely but it's not impossible, certainly not in a case where you've never concealed from anyone that Hugh is adopted. Such odd coincidences do occur and that one certainly can't be ruled out.'

'But I thought you said it was billions to one,' said Mary.

'Oh, no,' said Mr Luttrell. 'What I say would be a billion to one chance is that the child's father, or someone who knew the child's father, casually wandering down your road should by chance stumble on the child and you. That is a virtual impossibility. We can rule it out.'

'Then this man is the father, or someone who knows him?'

'Not necessarily by any means. There are several possibilities. One is that he's a lunatic. That he makes a habit of chatting to strangers, finding out something about them and then frightening them if he can. For example, he may like frightening mothers of young children with the idea of kidnapping. Indeed, he tried that very thing on you. Then, when he found it was an adopted child, he thought it would be a good joke from his point of view to say he knew the father.'

'But he couldn't tell that we didn't know who the father was,' said Bill. 'If he was just a stray lunatic, for all he knew we'd adopted a child of a widow. Or we'd adopted the child of a brother or sister or a hundred and one other things of that kind.'

'Ah, but Mrs Woodthorpe did tell him the father wasn't known,' said Mr Luttrell.

'Suppose he is the father or comes from him, what can he do?'

'Absolutely and precisely nothing,' said Mr Luttrell.

'Then what's he after?'

'Unless,' went on Mr Luttrell, and paused for a moment. 'Unless,' he continued, 'there was, for example, an affiliation order against the father or something of that sort.'

'But there wasn't,' said Mary.

The solicitor thought for a moment.

'Of course,' he said, 'we only have the mother's word for that. I suppose it's conceivable that she was telling lies. But, if that was the case, I'd have expected something to happen before now.'

'Why?'

'Otherwise the father would be paying money every week for nothing. Incidentally, that's quite a comforting thought. Suppose there was an affiliation order, but the mother lied about it in order to get rid of the child *and* keep the money, the father may have become suspicious and started to make enquiries. If he could prove adoption his liability would be at an end.'

'But surely,' said Bill, 'that would be a very odd way to go about it. Wouldn't he tell the Court where he paid the money what he suspected, and ask that the child should be produced? That would finish the mother. No need to go hunting round for the child.'

'True enough,' said Mr Luttrell. 'By the same token the mother might want to borrow the child to show at the Magistrates' court. But that's really very far-fetched. We can debate about this for hours, but we shan't get any further until the man has told us a bit more. You'll have to stop him and ask him.'

'Suppose he never comes again?'

'Then you've nothing to worry about. But, unless he's just a lunatic, he or someone else will come again. And you must tackle him about it. Better still, your husband should.'

'But I can't stay at home every day,' said Bill.

'I quite see that, but perhaps you could manage a fortnight, say. If he doesn't come within that time, I doubt if he'll call again. If he does come, find out what he wants and what he knows, and come and tell me.'

'You don't think we should go to the police?'

'Certainly not at the moment. As far as one can tell, the man hasn't broken the law in any way. He has simply said that he knows the father of your child. True or false, it isn't a crime to say that.'

'Mr Luttrell,' said Mary, 'if there was an affiliation order, what could the father do?'

'Nothing very effective, I'm sure,' said Mr Luttrell.

'But you said he couldn't do anything unless there was an affiliation order. That means he could do something if there was.'

'Well, strictly speaking,' said Mr Luttrell, 'a man who is liable to contribute to the maintenance of a child by virtue of an order or agreement is entitled to be heard on the question whether or not an adoption order should be made. If there was an affiliation order, the father was entitled to be served with your application for adoption and to appear before the judge and say why he objected, if he did object. Strictly speaking, then, if he wasn't served with your application he could, I suppose, apply to have the order set aside.'

'The affiliation order?'

'No, I mean the adoption order. Hold on a minute, Mrs Woodthorpe … it's not …'

Mary had nearly fainted. When she recovered, she said: 'But I thought you said there was nothing effective he could do. And now you say he could set aside the adoption order. That means we'd lose Hugh. I can't lose him. I won't.'

'Please don't get too distressed, Mrs Woodthorpe. Although technically he might be able to apply to set the adoption order aside, unless he could show some good reason why it should not be made again, the Court in order to avoid circuity of action would refuse to set aside the order.'

'I just don't understand,' said Mary. 'And now you're starting to use long words. Circu – something, what on earth does that mean? And why wasn't all this thought of long ago? Why wasn't the father found and asked about it before we had the order?'

'Now, please don't get upset,' said Mr Luttrell. 'I'm sure you'll have nothing to worry about.'

'Nothing to worry about!' said Mary. 'My whole life, our whole lives are concerned, and you say there's nothing to worry about. I'm beginning to think that this easy judge what's-his-name, who didn't worry about technicalities, wasn't such a good idea after all.'

'I've never had a case like this before,' said Mr Luttrell.

'Well, you've got one now,' said Mary. 'At least I'm not sure that you have. Perhaps we should go …'

'Now, darling,' said Bill, 'Mr Luttrell is doing his best for us, and has done it all along. Let's do what he says and see what this fellow's really after.'

'I'm sorry,' said Mary. 'I didn't mean to be rude. But I just can't tell you how I feel.'

'I quite understand,' said Mr Luttrell. 'Give me a ring as soon as you have any more news.'

They left the office and went home, Bill comforting Mary as best he could.

'I'm sure we're making too heavy weather of this,' he said. 'It's so easy to imagine things. Anyway, I'll stay at home for a fortnight.'

A few days later Mary, who had watched for the man every day and almost all day, saw him coming down the street. She told Bill, who had waited inside the house. The man came along, took off his hat to Mary, smiled, and went on. Mary went inside the house at once.

'Quick, after him,' she said.

Bill went out and soon caught him up.

'Excuse me,' he said. 'Might I have a word with you?'

The man stopped and turned to look at Bill.

'Yes?' he said enquiringly.

'You've been talking to my wife,' he said.

'The charming young woman just down the road with the just as charming child? Yes, certainly. But I assure you I don't know her and there was nothing improper about it.'

'You told her you know the father of the child.'

'Yes,' said the man.

'How do you know him?'

'Before I answer that, would you tell me any reason why I should?'

'You've frightened the life out of my wife, and I'm entitled to know.'

'Frightened the life out of her? Quite unintentional, I assure you. I'm so sorry. Please assure her that I didn't mean to.'

'Who are you, and what d'you want?'

'Why on earth should I say who I am and what I want? My car hasn't run into yours or anything like that. Why should I give you my name and address? I don't mind telling you my wants, though. The same as nearly everyone else's. Now, if you'll excuse me, I'd like to continue my stroll.'

'I must know what you want and what you know.'

'Must you?' said the man, and started to walk on.

Bill followed him.

'Would you mind?' said the man, 'or must I call a policeman? You're beginning to annoy me.'

'I'm sorry,' said Bill. 'I don't want to annoy you. I just want to understand. My wife is desperately worried. Surely you'd want to help her?'

The man stopped.

'Well,' he said, 'that's rather a different attitude to adopt. To help a lady in distress is one thing. To be bullied is another.' He paused for a moment and then repeated quickly, 'I won't be bullied.'

'Perhaps you'd be very kind and come back with me, then,' said Bill. 'Come and have a chat and a drink.'

'Now, that's very civil of you. I should enjoy it. And to see your wife again. I do congratulate you on her. You're very lucky.'

Bill rather preferred the man's aggressive to his oily attitude, but he could see that he would get nothing out of him unless he played the game the man's way. So he gave in with as good a grace as possible.

They walked back to the house. Mary was waiting for them.

'I'm afraid I can't introduce you,' began Bill, 'but ...'

'Baines,' said the man. 'Archie Baines. Baines is all right, but I hate Archie. It's not even Archibald. Believe it or not, I was christened Archie.'

'May I introduce Mr Baines,' said Bill. 'My wife.'

'We're old friends,' said the man. 'How nice to see you again. I've enjoyed our chats.'

'I've asked Mr Baines to have a glass of sherry with us.'

She could not say: 'How nice.' So she said nothing and led them into the sitting-room, where she produced sherry and glasses.

'Your health,' said the man, 'and the young man's.'

They each sipped their sherry.

'And now,' said the man, 'I believe I can be of some service to you. Pray tell me how.'

No one spoke for several seconds. Then Mary said: 'You said the other day that you know Hugh's father. Is that a fact?'

'It would be a very strange thing to say if it weren't.' He paused. 'Yes, it's a fact,' he added.

'Who is he?'

'I'm not sure that I ought to tell you. It might be betraying a professional confidence.'

'Are you his – his lawyer, then?'

'Oh dear no. But thank you for the compliment, if indeed it is a compliment to look like a lawyer.'

'His accountant?'

'No such luck. If you can call mine a profession it's pretty low in the hierarchy of professions. We have no institute or institution, not even an association. I'm an enquiry agent, as a matter of fact. Even bookmakers have an association. Several, in fact. Perhaps we will one day. How does RIPI sound? The Royal Institution of Private Investigators. I like the RIP anyway. We're such peaceable fellows.'

'You're an enquiry agent, then?' asked Bill.

'Not entirely – but in this matter, yes.'

'Is Hugh anything to do with your enquiries?'

'Yes and no.'

'Could you explain what you mean?'

'I'm afraid not. Not at the moment, anyway. What excellent sherry.'

An awkward silence followed. Mary hardly dared to ask the questions she wanted to ask, lest the answers should make things worse. But worst of all was not to know.

Eventually she started. 'Does he – does he – the father I mean, know about Hugh?'

'Well – a father ought to, shouldn't he?'

'D'you mean he knows that Hugh is ours?'

'I didn't say that. You asked if the father knew about Hugh. Well, if you have a baby a father should know it – not as well as the mother, of course, but well enough.'

'He might not. I mean, if he just met a girl at a dance.'

'I see what you mean. Just a casual one-day affair. Is that what you mean?'

'Yes.'

'You think that's the father in this case?'

'We were told so.'

'I see.'

'Isn't it correct?'

'Let me think,' said the man. 'Ought I to tell you or would it be a breach of our code? In spite of the absence of any RIPI we have a strict code, you know. I know a lot of people don't like us and judges sometimes say the most horrible things about us. We have, of course, some black sheep among us, but we're certainly not as bad as people think. For example, we rarely invent evidence. Certainly not if we can get it the proper way. No short cuts, I mean. Of course, if we come up against an absolutely blank wall – well, human nature being what it is, we might stretch a point. But what were you asking me? I'm digressing. You don't want an exposition of the morals of an enquiry agent, do you?'

'We asked if Hugh was the result of a casual affair,' said Bill.

'I really don't see why I shouldn't tell you that. No, for the life of me I don't. But I must be sure about it. Can't recall the spoken word, you know. Once I've said it, I've said it. Once you know it, you know it. No use telling my client I'm sorry, I didn't mean to and all that, if he's told me not to tell you. Now has he? It should be in my files, if he has. But I haven't got them here. Perhaps after all I'd better let the matter stand over. I'll be passing here again, no doubt, and you could ask me then. I must make a point of looking up my files. How to remember?'

He took out a handkerchief and tied a knot in it.

'An old method,' he said, 'but I find it pretty effective. Unless, of course, I lose the thing, or throw it in the laundry basket as soon as I get home. Now, I really mustn't keep you any more. It's been so kind of you.'

'But why are you interested in the child?' asked Bill.

'It's a nice child.'

'There are plenty of those.'

'That's a great comfort, isn't it?' said the man. 'Plenty more where that came from.'

Mary went white. She clenched a chair with her hands and almost whispered: 'Are you trying to take Hugh away from us?'

'Me personally? Good gracious no. What should I want with a baby? No offence, and all that, but I don't want him.'

'Does the father?'

'I suppose he might, if he knew.'

'Then he doesn't know.'

'Good gracious no. Not yet. I'm very particular about giving information. Got to be certain first, haven't I? Suppose I told a man it was his child and it wasn't, I'd be for it, wouldn't I? I'll tell you something. Don't you envy my self-control? Here am I being cross-examined up hill and down dale by you two – in the nicest possible way, of course. But it's I really who ought to be asking you questions. And I haven't asked a thing. That's pretty good, isn't it? Now, I really must be going. No, please don't show me out. No doubt I'll be seeing you again soon.'

He got up, took his hat and went quickly out of the door, out of the gate and up the street.

CHAPTER SEVEN

The Stranger Calls Again

As soon as he had gone Mary clung to Bill for help. For a short time she sobbed uncontrollably. He held her in silence. After she had recovered, he said, 'We must go to Luttrell at once.'

'What can he do?'

'At least advise us on the next step.'

They were not able to arrange an interview with the solicitor until the next morning, but he saw them then and they told him what had happened.

'One thing is certain, I'm afraid,' he said. 'He will come again.'

'What is his object?'

'Well, I can't know for certain and I don't want to alarm you but, I think, blackmail.'

'Blackmail?'

'Mind you, as I say, there's nothing certain about it, but what I think is this. This man, whether he's the father himself or, as he says, an enquiry agent, or neither, has found out that you adopted Hugh. It's possible he knows no more than that.'

'But surely …'

'Nearly every adoptive parent can be scared at the thought of losing the child. However much he or she may

55

have been advised that the adoption order is binding, once the possibility of there having been some legal hitch gets into their mind, many of them would become terrified at the thought of losing the child. A happily married couple who have their own child cannot be deprived of it by law, unless they ill-treat it. So you can't blackmail ordinary parents, except by kidnapping. And that's a very difficult and dangerous operation. But an adopted child is another matter. Not even a lawyer knows all the law or anything like it. How can a layman tell what it is? I'll guarantee that, if you took the simplest case, for example, where both the father and mother of the child had consented in writing to the adoption, the adoptive parents would at least be shaken by being told by a stranger that the adoption order wasn't binding and could be set aside. Of course, in such a case they'd go to their lawyers and find that it was just a try-on, as it may well be here. But they'd be shaken at first. First-class material for blackmail. This man may make a habit of it.'

'But surely he'd have been caught long ago,' said Bill. 'When the people he'd started on found out that they'd nothing to fear, they'd go to the police and he'd be trapped.'

'That's true,' said Mr Luttrell, 'but you may be his first victims.'

'Mr Luttrell,' said Mary, 'if this man is going to try to blackmail us, and if we have him prosecuted, can you assure me absolutely that there is no chance, no chance whatever of our losing Hugh?'

'If he's the father, none whatever.'

'Then, if he's not the father?'

Mr Luttrell thought for a short time. His very silence conveyed his answer to Mary. Before he could speak, she said: 'Then there is a chance, if he's not the father?'

56

'Mrs Woodthorpe, I hate to see anyone as anxious as you are, but I should not be doing my duty if I simply said that there was no chance whatever. I think it highly improbable, but I cannot in all honesty say that there is no chance whatever. I'm afraid that I'm beginning to agree with what you said at an earlier interview. It may well have been a pity this case didn't come before Judge Hazlewell.'

'Exactly what difference would it have made?' asked Bill.

'Well, he would have insisted on careful enquiries being made about the father. He wouldn't have accepted the mere word of the mother. The enquiries might have led nowhere and the mother might have stuck to her story. If that had happened, we'd be no better off than we are now, though you would have had the consolation – such as it would have been – that everything had been done to prevent this situation arising. But I have to admit that, in the majority of cases, where Judge Hazlewell isn't satisfied with the mother's story, the truth is arrived at before the order is made and the father is found.'

'And what difference would that have made?'

'It would have meant that either the father consented to the adoption, in which case he couldn't make trouble afterwards, or that he objected to it. If he had objected, his objections would have been gone into fully then. If the judge had rejected them, then, unless he appealed, the order would have been as foolproof as if he had not objected. If he had appealed and had his appeal dismissed, it would have been the same as if he had not appealed. If, however, the judge or the Court of Appeal had allowed his objection, and refused to make an adoption order, undoubtedly you would have suffered great distress. But the child would only have been with you then for a few months. I know that even then it would have been a terrible blow to you, but nothing compared with what it would be now.'

'Why d'you tell us all this now?' asked Bill. 'Why not when we first came to you?'

'A very fair question,' said Mr Luttrell. 'And this is the answer. It is perfectly true that, before Judge Hazlewell makes an adoption order, he tries to tie up all the loose ends and to ensure that a situation like this can never arise.'

'Then surely it would have been better ...'

'Please let me finish,' said Mr Luttrell. 'The reason that I advised you to have the case heard before the other judge is this. In the first place I knew that you, like every other adopting mother, wanted the order made as quickly as possible. I knew, too, that any adjournment of the case would inevitably have made you anxious and unhappy. That's true, isn't it?'

'Yes,' said Bill, 'that is quite true.'

'Well now, I can assure you that, although, as I said, Judge Hazlewell's methods do often result in a putative father being found, I have never yet known a case where, when found, he objected. Sometimes he denied the paternity, which was just as good as a consent. Sometimes he was very angry at being found, but on no single occasion, and my experience is considerable, has he attempted to prevent the making of an adoption order. I need hardly tell you also that I have never come across a case like yours before. Naturally, in future ...'

But Mary broke in: 'In future! What does that matter to us?'

'You're quite right, Mrs Woodthorpe. My actions in the future are no consolation to you. But you're entitled to an explanation from me and I'm entitled to give it. I had to weigh up your unhappiness and anxiety if the case had been adjourned, against the possibility that this might happen, something which to my knowledge had never happened before. It was in the highest degree unlikely that the father, if found, would object. We still have no reason to think that he will object. It was also in the highest degree unlikely that any blackmailer would ever be able to find out who you were or where the child was. I can only say that, although with this present experience of yours before me, I should warn the client of this most unlikely possibility, I should be perfectly prepared to do the same again unless the client, after being warned by me, preferred to take no chances.'

'Shouldn't you have told us of the risk, however small, of going before Judge Bramcote?' asked Bill.

'It's easy to be wise after the event. Certainly I shall tell my clients in the future. But I must admit that I never contemplated such a possibility. It's a chance in a hundred thousand. I considered Judge Hazlewell to be too pernickety. I freely admit that he has himself given as a reason for the attitude he adopts the possibility that something like this might happen. But I'm afraid that, as a result of my experience that it never *did* happen, I discounted the possibility.'

'So what do we do now?' asked Bill.

'Well, if it's blackmail, we must go to the police,' said Mr Luttrell, 'but there isn't really any evidence of this at the moment. What you'll have to do is to let him talk and, as soon as any suggestion of money comes into it, come back to me, or go straight to the police yourselves.'

'And what will they do?' asked Mary.

'They'll set a trap for the man, with your co-operation. And, if he's caught, he'll go to prison for a long time, as he'll richly deserve.'

'Won't he have to be tried first?'

'Of course.'

'And we'll have to give evidence?'

'I'm afraid so.'

'Thank you for being so frank, Mr Luttrell,' said Bill, but Mary said nothing.

After a little further conversation Bill and Mary went home.

'I'm sure it'll be all right,' said Bill, 'and I'm longing to see that chap in jail.'

'I don't mind whether he goes to prison or not, so long as we're safe with Hugh.'

'We're certain to be,' said Bill. 'I know what a strain it is on you, darling, but, believe me, it'll be all right. Would you like me to stay at home for a fortnight again?'

'No,' said Mary, 'I don't think so. Now that I've met him with you, I think I can manage.'

'Ring me as soon as he's left, then,' said Bill.

'You bet,' said Mary.

A week went by and Mary did not ring Bill. A fortnight, and still she didn't.

'I think he's given up,' said Bill. 'Give me a kiss and look happy.'

She kissed him and tried to look happy, but it was not a great success.

A month went by. Mary looked worse and worse. Three months and she was no better.

'Look, darling,' said Bill, 'we'll go for a holiday. You can't forget about that horrible man, but he's left us now for good. Hugh's our own forever. Why so miserable? You've both of us.'

Mary burst into tears.

'Darling, what is it?'

'Nothing, really. I'm so happy, I expect.'

But she certainly did not look it.

Bill returned to the holiday theme.

'Let's go somewhere really far away. I'll take three weeks off. Now. Anywhere you like. You go and make the reservations. Anywhere at all. Don't bother what it costs.'

'It sounds wonderful,' said Mary. 'I shall love it. Just to get away. With you and Hugh. It's sweet of you. Three whole weeks.'

She seemed to look happier than she had for a long time. Just before he left she said: 'Will you give me a cheque for the deposits?'

'You pay it, darling, and I'll give it you back.'

'All right,' she said, and then added: 'As a matter of fact, I'm a bit low in my account at the moment. I would prefer to have a cheque.'

'Of course, but I haven't one with me. I'll bring one home tonight and you can go tomorrow.'

On the way to the office, happy that Mary had for once looked more herself, Bill suddenly thought about her saying that her account was a bit low. That's very odd, he said to himself. He made Mary a substantial quarterly allowance and in addition she had quite a reasonable income of her own. She spent quite a lot on clothes, but she had never appeared short of money before. A horrible thought crossed his mind. He went to the office, collected his cheque book and went straight home.

He found Mary in tears.

'Is this what you do all day?' he asked.

She nodded miserably.

'I've brought my cheque book,' he said, 'and not, I think, before it's time.'

She looked at him sharply. He had never seen her look quite like that.

'You've been buying him off, haven't you?' he said.

61

She sobbed. The relief that he knew was coupled with fear of what he might do. He took her on his lap, like a child, and let her sob on to his shoulder. When she was quiet, he said softly: 'Now tell me all about it, darling.'

'You won't do anything?' she asked fearfully. 'Promise.'

'Darling, I won't do anything that won't help. That I promise.'

'But you'll think it'll help and you'll be wrong … and – and – '

She burst into tears again. Then she steadied herself.

'I want to tell you, oh so much. It's been terrible. But you must promise first.'

'All right,' he said, 'I promise.'

'He's been coming here ever since that day.'

'Did he ask for anything?'

'Not really. I offered.'

'What did you say?'

'I said it would be worth a lot to me if the father never knew. Then he said he had his duty to do. So I said: "Can't I employ you?" "As what?" he said. "As an anti-enquiry agent," I said. "That's a novel proposition," he said. "What are your usual charges?" I asked. "I haven't any usual charges," he said; "it all depends on the case and the client." "Well, the case is that I don't want the father to know and the client is me." '

'How much have you paid him altogether?'

'Over £700.'

'It's just as well I came home.'

'But you've promised not to do anything.'

'Then what's the good of my coming home?'

'What's the good? Why, you can help me pay now. Now that you know, everything's going to be all right.'

For once Mary looked almost cheerful.

'You mean,' said Bill, 'that we're to go on paying this fellow for the rest of our lives?'

'Gracious no,' said Mary, 'only till Hugh is sixteen. I'd got it worked out that with my capital I could manage for seven years. But then his charges started to go up. But, now you're in it too, it'll be fine.'

'D'you realise what sort of a man we're dealing with? By the time Hugh is sixteen we'll probably have paid him at least twenty-five thousand pounds.'

Mary smiled cheerfully.

'But you've got more than that, darling. And you can cut down my allowance. Oh, this is wonderful. I am lucky to have such a husband. I'm sure a lot wouldn't stand for it.'

Bill looked blankly in front of him. Mary really meant it. He had a good income and about £40,000 capital. What was £25,000 compared with Mary's happiness? It was an awful lot of money to pay to a scoundrel but, if it would make Mary happy, he'd do it. And what was the alternative? A prosecution. The father would then be almost certain to learn, and what would happen then? No one could tell. Mr Luttrell's talk about circuity of action had been almost as baffling to him as it was to Mary. But, on the other hand, the father mightn't be interested at all. This might be just a blackmailer who'd accidentally got on to a good thing, and was pretending he knew the father and that the father wanted enquiries made. To pay £25,000 to prevent an application to set aside the adoption order was one thing. He would do it cheerfully. But to be swindled out of it for nothing was another matter. Bill had an idea. It was not breaking his promise to Mary to keep it to himself.

'I'm so glad you've told me,' said Bill. 'Of course Hugh is worth £25,000 and more – all I've got, in fact.'

'Darling,' she said, and for the first time for months smiled really happily.

'Now, I'm not going to let you bear the burden any longer. I'm going to pay the chap myself. I may even be able to do a deal with him. A lump sum not to come again.'

'Wonderful,' said Mary.

'When will he be here again?' he asked.

'Next Friday, I expect,' she said.

'Right,' said Bill, 'I'll be here.'

'You have promised not to tell, haven't you? Not Mr Luttrell, or the police, or anyone?'

'Of course,' he said.

He waited patiently for next Friday.

CHAPTER EIGHT

A Nice Round Sum

The man who called himself Baines arrived almost exactly when he was expected. He had begun to look forward to these interviews. He found the exercise of power exciting and the result of such exercise most remunerative. But greed is the ruin of the criminal. He comes too often or asks too much. In blackmail it seems so easy. Why on earth should one labour with one's body or mind seven or eight hours a day to gain a comparatively small sum when, by the sweet use of power, one can get more in a quarter of an hour?

It was upon this known greed of blackmailers that Bill was banking. He realised, of course, that he would have to be most discreet when he first came upon the scene, or the man might expect a trap, take fright and disappear. Though his disappearance would be a considerable gain, there would always remain with Mary a lingering fear until the exact amount of the man's knowledge, and any purpose for which he had come other than blackmail, was known. So he must play him gently until the right moment.

Mary let the man in and took him to the sitting-room. He did not give any sign that he was affected by seeing Bill.

He was too controlled for that, but he must have been shocked.

'Good morning,' said Bill.

'Nice to see you again,' said the man.

'I'd rather like to have a talk with you alone for a few minutes,' said Bill. 'Darling, will you go and play with Hugh in the front?'

Mary and Hugh went outside where they were in full view of the men inside the room. Bill closed the window. The windows were double-glazed and this ensured that they could not be heard. It was important to do this openly, so that the man's suspicions of a trap might be allayed. After all, a husband and wife are two witnesses, a husband only one. Unless there were someone concealed somewhere, or unless there were microphones in the room, the suggested interview must look reasonably innocent.

'Well now,' said Bill, 'I understand my wife has been employing you. A sort of counter espionage.'

'You can put it that way, but I haven't asked her for a penny.'

'Who said you had? I'm quite satisfied that whatever she's paid you was paid by her entirely voluntarily. Indeed, it was her suggestion.'

'I'm glad you recognise that.'

'Of course.'

'Then what is it you want?'

'Just a business talk. I wanted to see if we could do a deal for a lump sum. For one thing, I don't think it does Mary any good having these regular meetings. For another it's getting expensive. Now, I'm not rich but I'm not poor, and I'd be prepared to settle once and for all for a largish cash payment. Let me make it plain that I'm offering this. You're not asking it.'

'Would you put that in writing?'

'Willingly, if we can agree on a figure. Now I look at it this way,' said Bill. 'I'm not an actuary but it's possible to look at things actuarially from a layman's point of view. Say we want to cover the next twelve years. At the present rate of striking I'd say that Mary would be paying you between £1,000 and £2,000 a year. What would you say to £20,000?'

Once again the man was able to prevent his true reactions to the suggestion being noticed.

'You were saying?' he said.

'£25,000,' said Bill.

'I didn't quite catch,' said the man.

'I don't think I could go above £30,000.'

'Did you say thirty, or forty?'

'Forty.'

'I think that might be arranged,' said the man.

He would have been very content with a suggestion of £5,000. After all, he could always come again when that was exhausted. He'd willingly have stayed away for a month or two, or even more, for £5,000. But, when Bill mentioned £20,000, he could see a completely different life opening for him. And, if a man will start the bidding at £20,000, he'll go a long way beyond. With £40,000 he could even afford to start life abroad and really drop the Woodthorpes. It was a chance too good to be missed. He decided he would put it up to £50,000. If a man will pay forty, he'll pay fifty. And fifty was a nice round sum. Bill allowed himself to be raised to £50,000.

'I'll have to sell some securities,' he said, 'but I can let you have it in a week, I should think. And I dare say you'd like that little bit I said I'd put in writing.'

'Thank you. There's no need to mention the amount.'

'Of course not,' said Bill. 'How will this do? "Any sums handed by me or my wife to Mr Baines – " I forget your Christian name.'

'Never mind. Baines will do.'

' "Handed by me to Mr Baines were entirely our own idea and handed over absolutely voluntarily." How's that?'

'Yes, I think that will do.'

Bill wrote it out on a piece of paper and handed it over.

'Now perhaps we'll have my wife in and tell her we've settled everything.'

He called Mary and she came at once.

'Mr Baines and I have settled the matter once and for all, darling,' he said.

'Oh – good,' said Mary.

'I'm going to give him a lump sum in about a week. I'll give it to you and you can hand it to him.'

'I'm so glad,' said Mary. 'Then it's all settled.'

'Indeed yes,' said the man. 'I must admit that I've enjoyed our chats. But all good things come to an end. But there'll be one more. In a week, I think you said? I'll be here. Same time. Good day,' and he left.

'You are clever,' said Mary. 'How much are you going to give him?'

Bill hesitated.

'I'm afraid it's rather a lot. He fairly put the screw on me and there was nothing I could do but agree.'

'But how much? Over £1,000?'

'Hold tight, darling. And let me say first I don't grudge a penny of it, if it makes you happy.'

'How much?' said Mary.

'Er – £50,000,' said Bill.

'You're joking.'

'I'm afraid not.'

'But it's impossible. It'll be pretty well all you have.'

'Hugh and you are worth much more, and I've got you both.'

'But I can't let you do it. £50,000! It's impossible. What an utter blackguard! Oh, I could bite him, I hate him so!'

'I doubt if he'd taste very nice.'

'But what can we do? I'm not going to let you be ruined. How can we prevent it?'

'Well, of course, we could – but you hate the idea so.'

'Could what? Go to the police, you mean?'

'Well, we could, but I wouldn't dream of it, unless you wanted to.'

'Oh, darling, it's so awful,' said Mary. 'But you're quite right. We must go to them. I can't think why I was so silly before. They'll let us keep Hugh, won't they?'

'Of course they will. I don't suppose he even knows the father. And, even if he does, the father doesn't want Hugh or he'd have done something before.'

Mary brightened at that.

'Yes, I suppose he would. He could have gone to the Court, couldn't he?'

'He'd have to find out which it was, but he could do that quite easily from the mother. I'm sure there's nothing to worry about except this ruffian, and we'll soon put him where he belongs. Let's go round to the police now.'

Bill thought it as well to get things started, in case Mary should change her mind. However, she showed no signs of doing so and, within a few days, a reception committee had been arranged for Archie Baines.

CHAPTER NINE

The Final Call

Meanwhile the man in question was getting more and more elated. He was a petty criminal, one of whose parents appeared in *Who's Who*. He had been sent to a public school but allowed to leave early, because he was ambitious to 'get on'. As his father had had practically no education but had at a comparatively early age made vast sums of money in business of one kind or another, he had no objection to his son trying to do the same. But neither he nor his wife gave any time to their boy's upbringing. They had none to give, the father being occupied in making more and more money (with no obvious object except possibly a barony), the mother being equally occupied in organising social functions for various charities. All they had done for Eric was to give him money, and, when he had disgraced them sufficiently often, they paid him off on condition that he changed his name to Smith. The parting was on. a purely business basis.

'As my son,' said Eric's father, 'I won't give you another penny. As Eric Smith – deed poll and all that and I'll want to see it first – as Eric Smith you can have £5,000, and get out.'

Eric produced the deed poll and his father produced the £5,000. It seemed a lot at the time but it was not long before he needed more. So he traded on an educated accent – the only thing he had acquired at school – and his reasonable good looks, and started to make money how he could.

When Eric Smith was stated in the newspapers to have been sent to prison it meant nothing to his parents. It mightn't even be their son. There must be a good many Eric Smiths in prison. But he did not often find his way into the national press, his crimes being of no general interest.

And now he was really going to crown his career. £50,000, and in one venture. He could start life all over again. He'd go into a legitimate business somewhere. Perhaps even marry and settle down. He conjured up wonderful visions of the future. Cars, women, hotels, sandy beaches, luxury air travel – the lot. He hadn't done so badly after all. What a bit of luck that he'd been told about the Woodthorpes. He never dreamed it would be so easy. If ever there was a piece of cake, this was it. He even thought of sending his father £5,000 with a rude message. On second thoughts he decided to send the rude message only. From the most expensive hotel in the Bahamas. But just a letter wouldn't do, or his father would think he'd simply got a job in the hotel or something. Anyway, that could take care of itself. In a week's time he'd have £50,000. Almost as much as his father had made at the same age.

He could hardly wait for the week to end. He even thought of paying a mid-week call just to encourage the lady. There was no doubt she was terrified of him. It gave him a pleasant tingling sensation when he remembered his visits and thought of her white, frightened face. He

could have made her do anything. And all for a stupid
little toddler who might easily be killed in a road accident
within a year or two. Or have pneumonia and die. Having
regard to his own home, it was not surprising that Eric was
contemptuous of mother love. Mary's husband hadn't
appeared frightened, but obviously he wanted to protect
his wife. Perhaps he should have asked for £75,000, or
even £100,000. He'd got the chap up to £50,000 pretty
quickly. And without asking for a penny. Yes, he thought,
it's a pity I didn't run him up a bit more. 'Perhaps I can
still. But perhaps it's better not to. Every man must have
his limit, and, if you go beyond it, he may go for the
police. But she'd never let him, he told himself. He had
quite cleverly, without actually referring to the police,
made it quite plain to Mary that, if she went for help, she'd
stand a good chance of losing Hugh. He thought back on
it. He'd really been very clever. Not a threat, not a demand.
Should he put them up to £100,000? Take the £50,000
and say that next week there must be another? It was
deliciously tempting. He'd gone up so easily to fifty, he
must be a very rich man. What's another fifty to a
millionaire? But then he told himself that the
Woodthorpes' road and house, though pleasant, did not
look as though they were connected with a millionaire.
No, he mustn't be greedy. And, after all, he'd got them up
from twenty to fifty thousand. Not bad for a tyro.
Blackmail was quite new to him. How some of the petty
criminals he'd met would have envied him. (They might
have but, oddly enough, the hardened big-time criminal
would have despised him. Blackmail is not a popular
crime with the professional criminal. Not with one of
class, anyway.)

Gradually the week went by and at last the great day
came. He dressed particularly well that day. He'd do it in

style. Itching to have his hands on the £50,000, he nevertheless managed to stroll down the road as though he were in no hurry at all. He got a pleasant sensation out of controlling himself, different from the sensation of power over Mary but in a way akin to it. He slowed down even more. It was like a small boy counting fifty before he eats a beautiful ice.

At last he reached the house and Mary was waiting for him.

'My husband's at the office,' she said. 'He hoped you wouldn't mind.'

Mind, he thought, that's a good one.

'Not at all,' he said. 'I've enjoyed our little conversations solo.'

'Then do sit down and have a glass of sherry.'

This was not at all what he wanted. Squeezing Mary in the past for small sums was fun. But he wanted this £50,000 in his hands as quickly as possible. So that he could go home and count it, yes, and gloat over it. But it wouldn't do to appear too impatient.

'That's very kind,' he said, and sat down.

'There's just one thing,' said Mary, as she gave him the sherry, 'there really will be no chance of the father learning where Hugh is if we hire you as suggested?'

'You can forget all about the father. There is no father. Never was any father.'

Mary was startled.

'You mean you only made it up?'

'Good gracious no,' said Eric. 'All I mean is that, with me on your side, the only father this boy will ever know is at his office, and his name ... I'll give you one guess ... no, I won't, it's Woodthorpe.'

'Thank you,' said Mary. 'Then you'll certainly earn our most grateful thanks.'

73

A bit more than thanks, thought Eric, but it didn't do to say so.

'Don't mention it. It's just a business transaction.'

After a moment he added, when he found the delay becoming insupportable: 'Talking of which, I wonder ...'

He was very careful to use no words of demand. Just suppose they had gone to the police, he wasn't making any evidence against himself. At each interview he'd been careful to make any hint of money come from Mary. But now she was being difficult. Perhaps *she* was trying to get her money's worth. Trying to get him to beg like a dog. He'd once heard of a wife who'd made her husband do that when he wanted anything. But he mustn't fall for that. Just in case.

'Yes,' said Mary – 'you were wondering?'

'Just about our little bit of business.'

'Of course,' said Mary. '£50,000, it was.'

'Was it?' he said, in a tired voice, as though the whole thing was rather a bore. 'Was it, then? Well, if you say so, I'm quite happy about it.'

But although Mary mentioned the money, she made no attempt to get it. He looked round the room. There was a fat envelope on the desk. But not fat enough. If it was all in fivers, then there'd be 10,000 of them. Quite a package. He had asked for some pound notes, but he hadn't pressed it too hard in case it made them think he was frightened. But fivers would be all right, if you were careful. All the same he'd brought a suitcase in case it was only partly in fivers.

'Before you go,' said Mary, 'I wonder if you'd tell me something about the father?'

A sudden thought occurred to him.

'I might get you some information about him, but I'd have to pay for it.'

'I see,' said Mary. 'I'm afraid we can't run to any more.'

Oh well, he thought, perhaps I was right not to be greedy. But when is she going to cough it up? I'm tired of this.

'Nice little place you have here,' he forced himself to say.

'You still like it,' she said. 'I'm glad. We do. But is there nothing you already know about the father which you can tell me? After all, it won't cost you anything to tell me what you know. And how did you find out that we had his child?'

'That would be telling,' said Eric.

'Of course,' said Mary, 'and I do wish you'd tell me.'

'Sorry, Mrs Woodthorpe,' said Eric. 'I keep faith with all my clients. I'll keep faith with you by concealing your address and identity, and I'll keep faith with my other client by doing exactly the same for him. What could be fairer?'

'Very well,' said Mary. 'Now I mustn't keep you any more. Goodbye.'

She got up and held out her hand.

'But,' said Eric, 'but …'

'Yes?' said Mary.

'There was a parcel, wasn't there?'

'Of course, how stupid of me. It's in the hall. In brown paper. Perhaps you'd pick it up as you go out. Goodbye again.'

She showed him out of the room, and there was the brown paper parcel. Just about the right size, he reckoned. Good. At last. I'd have burst if we'd gone on talking any longer. He picked it up, put it in his suitcase and walked out of the house. Now for home, he said to himself. And there's going to be no strolling back either. I want to get my hands on the stuff. There was no taxi in sight. So he would have to walk till he found one.

He had gone about two hundred yards when a police car stopped beside him and two officers got out.

'Excuse me, sir,' said one of them. 'Would you mind telling me what's in that suitcase?'

God! thought Eric. But thank Heaven I've made no demands. No threats. They can't get me for this. I've lost the £50,000. No Bahamas this time. But they're not going to get me.

'Certainly, officer,' he said as calmly and slowly as he could, though it was not too easy. 'I've got a parcel with £50,000 in notes in it. I'd rather not open it here for obvious reasons. Might blow away.'

'Perhaps you wouldn't mind coming to Scotland Yard, sir, and opening it there,' said the officer.

'Scotland Yard?' said Eric. 'What on earth for?'

'A complaint has been made that you demanded £50,000 from Mr and Mrs Woodthorpe with menaces.'

'Quite untrue,' said Eric. 'They offered it me quite voluntarily.'

'I must warn you, sir, that you needn't say anything further unless you wish to do so but that anything you do say will be taken down in writing and may be given in evidence if you are charged with an offence.'

'And if I refuse?'

'Then I shall get a warrant for your arrest.'

'Get one if you like,' said Eric. 'I've committed no offence, and I'll trouble you to let me go on my way.'

'Very good, sir, but I warn you that you'll be followed. So I shouldn't try to leave the country or hide. And I'll relieve you of that parcel, sir.'

'You'll do nothing of the sort,' said Eric. 'I know my rights. It's mine.'

'It's not yours, sir, as a matter of fact. It belongs to the Receiver for the Metropolitan Police, if you want to know.'

The inspector opened the suitcase and took out the parcel. 'If it's any consolation to you, sir,' he added, 'there's no money in it. Just paper and wood. It wouldn't be much use to you, sir, but in any event, as I told you, it belongs to the Metropolitan Police. However, as you won't come to Scotland Yard, I'm going to open it in your presence. The other officer will see that nothing blows away.'

Unhappily Eric watched the parcel opened and saw the wood and newspaper. All his dreams for the future had gone, but he'd now got to be pretty careful about the present. They'd put it across him if they could.

'Make a note of this, please, officer,' he said.

A notebook was immediately produced.

'I never demanded anything from Mr and Mrs Woodthorpe,' he dictated, 'and I never made any threat to either of them.'

The officer wrote it down.

'Would you care to sign it, sir?' he asked.

'I don't see why not,' said Eric, and signed the statement.

'Might we have your address, sir?'

Eric paused. He had thought of running away, but it was difficult to hide indefinitely and, if he were caught, it would look bad before a judge and jury. He gave it to them.

'Thank you, sir,' said the officer. 'We shall be arresting you quite soon.'

'And I shall be suing you for false arrest,' said Eric.

'I told you we're getting a warrant, sir. You'd have to sue the magistrate, and I think your solicitor will tell you that can't be done. I should see a solicitor, if I were you, sir. You'll need one. It's a very serious offence.'

'It's not an offence at all,' said Eric. 'Now, kindly let me go.'

CHAPTER TEN

Solicitor and Client

'Don't tell me,' said Mr Tewkesbury, as Eric was shown into his office. 'I never forget a face. Wish I could sometimes.'

Mr Tewkesbury was a remarkable man. He had performed an astonishing feat of walking on the legal tightrope for years. He drank. Not, as he said, because he had a compulsion to do so but because he liked it. He conducted his practice (almost entirely in the criminal courts) without any scruples at all. Not, as he said, because he could not have got on any other way but because it was easier. He was entirely amoral. Not, as he said, because he was born that way but because, after years of trying, he had at last managed to attain that happy state.

For a very long time the Law Society had watched Mr Tewkesbury's activities with anxiety, not to say distress. But they had never managed to find a reason for striking him off the rolls. Indeed they had in some ways consolidated his position. Mr Tewkesbury kept no clerks. He had one girl typist, who was replaced from time to time. The result was that his accounts had at one time been in a hopeless state of confusion. If the Law Society had left him long enough, they would in the end have found ample material to justify his removal from the rolls. But they wouldn't leave him alone. Twice he was brought before them for not keeping proper accounts. Once he was fined £250 and once he was suspended for six months. It was a fatal mistake. Mr Tewkesbury, who was an extremely able man with a first-rate classical education, saw through the alcoholic haze a red light. After his suspension was over he employed a one-time chartered accountant to come in once a week to keep him straight. That is to say, straight as far as accounts were concerned. And the Law Society had lost its opportunity.

As to his more serious professional misbehaviour, it was impossible to prove. Subornation of perjury, in which he specialised, is practically incapable of proof when it takes place in a solicitor's office. Normally it can only be proved by the perjurer, and such a person, even if willing to give evidence against his suborner (which would be most exceptional), does not make a very satisfactory witness. Incidentally, Mr Tewkesbury would never have accepted that his persuasion of a witness to tell a story more helpful to his client than his original one amounted to a crime. Subornation of perjury was just a pompous expression to cover up someone's dislike of losing a case. His philosophy was me first, my client next and the law can go to hell.

The reason that Mr Tewkesbury retained his practice in spite of his drunken habits was twofold. First, his ability. He could produce a very respectable alibi better than most men. Secondly, you never had to make an appointment to see him. You just dropped in. If someone was in front of you, you just waited your turn. If he was asleep, you woke him up. Consequently he had a large and disreputable clientele. Although a good deal of what he said when he was recovering from a heavy bout of drinking was nonsense, it was usually mixed with some excellent, if grossly improper, advice.

'Don't tell me,' he repeated. 'Kindly turn round, sir.'

Eric obeyed. Mr Tewkesbury thought. Finally he spoke.

"We have never met before,' he said.

'I was recommended – ' began Eric, but Mr Tewkesbury stopped him.

'No references given or required,' he said. 'Mutual trust. Have you twenty guineas?'

'Twenty?' said Eric, a little crestfallen.

'Ten will do to begin with,' said Mr Tewkesbury, and added cheerfully: 'But I'll have the coat off your back before I've finished with you. We lawyers! Keep away from us, my boy. Never get into the courts if you can help it. *Dulce et decorum est desipere in loco*. I seem to have got that wrong somehow. No matter. Ten guineas, I think you said.'

Eric produced ten pounds.

'Come on, my boy,' said Mr Tewkesbury. 'The machine doesn't work until all the money's in it. Automation!' he added. 'It's the curse of the age. But there it is, you've got to get used to it.'

Eric handed over a further ten shillings.

'Good,' said Mr Tewkesbury. 'Now we can talk. But just one moment.'

He rang a bell and a girl came in.

Mr Tewkesbury looked at her with surprise.

'What's your name, girl?' he asked. 'You weren't here yesterday. I never forget a face.'

'I'm Miss Harper,' said the girl.

'Miss Fiddlesticks,' said Mr Tewkesbury. 'You're Jane and not so plain Jane either, I'm glad to say. Get the usual at Roebuck's, please.'

He handed her three pound notes. His eyes followed her until she'd left the room. Then he turned to Eric.

'The face is different,' he said, 'but the behind's the same. And now, sir, what can I do for you? An alibi, was it?

I'll want something better than the wife, if possible. Wives are rather corny.'

'I don't want an alibi,' said Eric.

'I hope you've thought seriously about this,' said Mr Tewkesbury. 'If you admit being there, how do you account for your presence at midnight in the strong room of a bank where you had no account? I assume you had no account, sir. You may think that's easy to explain, sir, but take the advice of an older man, sir, it's not. At midday it might be easy, even shortly after closing time would not be impossible, but at midnight it takes a bit of laughing off.'

'I'm going to be charged with blackmail,' said Eric.

Mr Tewkesbury rose unsteadily and held out his hand.

'My dear sir,' he said, as he shook Eric's hand warmly, 'this is a pleasant change. I'm most grateful. Breaking and entering, false pretences, grievous bodily harm are all very much the same. But blackmail has a romantic air to it. And you can't blackmail anyone unless there's something black about them. What had this fellow done?'

Eric explained.

'But I never made a threat or a demand. Not once.'

'Pray don't excite yourself,' said Mr Tewkesbury. 'You don't have to say that to me. I want the facts. They're so much easier to manipulate if one knows what they are.'

'I assure you – ' said Eric, but Mr Tewkesbury interrupted, tapping the table impatiently with a pencil as he did so.

'Come, come, sir,' he said. 'What you say to me is in absolute confidence. Better than the seal of the confessional, I assure you.'

After more interruptions Eric managed to tell Mr Tewkesbury what had happened.

'Only paper and wood,' Mr Tewkesbury said sadly, but then brightened slightly. 'Paper to represent the Bar, no doubt,' he said, 'and wood the Bench.'

'I'll get off all right, won't I?' asked Eric a little anxiously.

'You haven't been charged yet,' said Mr Tewkesbury.

'But I'm sure I will be. Those chaps meant business.'

Mr Tewkesbury picked up a law book.

'Let me see,' he mused, 'the maximum penalty for the offence you're likely to be charged with is two years per offence. Lucky you didn't write a letter. That could be a life sentence for each offence. The way they sentence people today, you'd need to be a cat.'

'But I'm not guilty,' said Eric. 'I've never made a demand.'

'It's a pity you said you'd got £50,000 in that parcel. If only you'd said it was paper and wood.'

'But how could I? I didn't know,' said Eric.

'Well, you know now,' said Mr Tewkesbury. 'All the same, I'm afraid it's too late to change that one round. Pity.'

'I thought I was doing the right thing,' said Eric. 'If they'd opened it up and found £50,000 in it, I'd have been finished if I hadn't admitted it.'

'Next time,' said Mr Tewkesbury, 'admit nothing. Say you're taking it to a man. You'd been asked to fetch a parcel and were taking it to a man. His name? I call him George. Meet him in the market on Tuesdays. It was a Friday? All right. Fridays then. Will you go with us to find George? Of course, officer, delighted. You go to the market. No George. He must have heard the police were on to him and scarpered. Simple, my dear sir.'

'But Mr and Mrs Woodthorpe will say it was me.'

'Of course they will. Highly respectable witnesses. No good suggesting they're telling lies. But mistake – that's another matter. Both too anxious about the baby to remember exactly what was said. It was a transaction between them and George. You were just the innocent go-between. Exactly the same conversation but with the addition that you're carrying out instructions. But it's too late for that now.'

'But I never made a …'

'My dear sir, I am often drunk but never deaf. I've heard you say that a hundred times. No demand, no threats.'

'You don't seem to think much of that as a defence,' said Eric rather miserably.

'Frankly no,' said Mr Tewkesbury. 'But we'll do what we can with it. Next time come and see me first and I'll tell you what to say.'

'But won't I get off?' asked Eric.

'You can never be sure,' said Mr Tewkesbury. 'In the days of capital punishment I wrote an obituary for a client the day before the verdict. For *The Times*, you know. He was quite a well-known man. He was delighted with it when I showed it to him later, after he got off.'

'So there is a chance?'

'There's always a chance. But quite frankly, sir, I'd prefer to be where I am than where you're going to be.'

'You're not very comforting,' said Eric.

'Is that what the ten guineas was for?' asked Mr Tewkesbury. 'Comfort? That's easy. My dear sir, you will never be charged with this crime. At this present moment Mr and Mrs Woodthorpe are being removed to the mortuary after a car accident, and all the police officers in the case have been blown up by a bomb. Or, if that sounds a little unlikely, the Director of Public Prosecutions is at this very moment saying words to this effect: "Prosecute my old friend Eric Smith? Never. He very nearly saved my life in the last war. Enter a *nolle prosequi* at once, Smithers."

How will that do for ten guineas, sir? Two for the price of one, you might say. Feel better now, sir?'

Eric left Mr Tewkesbury in a very unhappy frame of mind. He had felt so confident that he had a good defence. But a solicitor could be wrong. And, to judge from the stench of whisky in Mr Tewkesbury's room, he could at the least have been confused. Perhaps the Woodthorpes had had a fatal accident. But that was too good to hope for. It was. He was arrested the next day.

CHAPTER ELEVEN

The Trial

So far from having an accident Mary and Bill were feeling much happier. It was true that they were not entirely out of the wood and it was possible that Hugh's father had some rights in the matter. But, if he had, he had himself given no sign that he was interested in Hugh. Why not, if he was? Moreover, with luck the blackmailer might give them the information they wanted, if not voluntarily while in prison, at any rate in the witness box.

In due course they attended a conference with a representative of the Director of Public Prosecutions. First of all, he assured them that they would be known as Mr and Mrs X, so that the prosecution would not be likely to do them any harm. Secondly, he said that, if the man pleaded *not guilty* and went into the witness box, he could be asked about Hugh's father.

Altogether it was a great relief to them both to have told the police everything. They had handed over the responsibility. And, as the days and weeks went by with no further calls by frightening strangers, their confidence increased more and more. It was unpleasant having to give evidence at the Magistrates' court, but no more than unpleasant. They were allowed to be called Mr and Mrs X, and the Press did not bother them unduly.

Eventually Eric came up for trial at the Old Bailey. He pleaded *not guilty* and Mary and Bill had to give evidence again. Their cross-examination was no great ordeal. It was plain that the defence was the absence of threat or demand. At the close of the case for the prosecution Eric gave evidence. This was the moment for which Mary and Bill had been waiting. Eric had made no statement while awaiting trial and he said nothing about Hugh's father in his examination-in-chief. Counsel for the Crown then rose to cross-examine and Mary and Bill listened intently.

'Do you really know the father of this boy?' asked counsel.

'I think so,' said Eric.

'You *think*?' said counsel. 'Either you do or you don't.'

'How can I *know* he was the father?' asked Eric. 'I wasn't present when the boy was born.'

'You're quite right,' said counsel. 'And even that wouldn't have told you. It was my fault. What you mean is that you have met a man who *said* he was the father?'

'Yes.'

'Where did you meet him?'

Before Eric could answer, his own counsel spoke quietly to his opponent.

'Don't answer that question for the moment, Mr Smith,' said counsel. 'Would your Lordship forgive me for a moment?'

The judge nodded, and there was a whispered conversation between the two counsel. To Mary and Bill's dismay, when they had finished prosecuting counsel went on: 'Thank you, my Lord. Did the father ever ask you to approach Mr or Mrs X?' Apparently he had completely abandoned the line of questioning which would show who the father was.

'No,' said Eric.

'Then why did you approach them?'

'I thought I might do them a good turn.'

'A good turn?'

'Yes.'

'In what way?'

'Well, I knew the father might go looking for the child.'

'How did you know that?'

'From what the father said.'

'And how could you help Mr and Mrs X?'

'By heading the father off, if he tried to find them. That's what they asked me to do. And they offered to pay me well to do it.'

'How could you head the father off?'

'By telling him I hadn't found the child, or by giving him misleading information.'

'By lying to him, in other words?'

'You can put it like that.'

'How would you put it?'

Eric was silent.

'Well, how *would* you put it?'

'Like I said.'

'You were being paid to tell lies to the father?'

'That's not illegal.'

'Never mind whether it's illegal or not. That is what you say happened. You were to receive £50,000 to tell lies to the father? That's your case, isn't it?'

'I suppose so.'

'Don't let's have any supposing about it. Is that not your case – that you were to be paid £50,000 for telling lies to the father?'

'If you like. But I never asked for the £50,000.'

'You asked for the parcel, did you not? You've heard the recording taken by the police of your last interview with

Mrs Woodthorpe – I mean Mrs X. That was your voice asking for the parcel, wasn't it?'

'I didn't ask for it.'

'You said "there was a parcel, wasn't there?" didn't you?'

'You've got the recording.'

'But that's what you said, isn't it?'

'Suppose it was?'

'By saying "there was a parcel, wasn't there?", didn't you mean to ask for the parcel?'

'I just said it.'

'I know, but if it wasn't asking for the parcel what did it mean? "There was a parcel, wasn't there?" repeated counsel. 'That meant, did it not, "please give me the parcel which you've previously arranged to give me"?'

'You can twist anything.'

'I hope I'm not but, if I am, you tell me what I'm twisting. Why did you refer to the parcel at all if it was not your object to get it?'

Eric did not answer.

'Hadn't you come to the house for the express purpose of getting the parcel?'

'Perhaps.'

'For what other reason had you come? To have a glass of sherry?'

'It's easy to be sarcastic from where you are,' said Eric. 'You wouldn't find it so pleasant from here.'

The judge did not intervene. He rather agreed with Eric. 'I'm sorry,' said counsel, 'but can you tell me any other object you had in coming to the house, except to get the parcel?'

Eric was silent again.

'May I take your silence to mean that you had no other object?'

'I suppose so.'

'Very well, then. Having no other object in coming to the house, except to collect the parcel, what else could you have meant when you said "there was a parcel, wasn't there?" except "please give me the parcel"?'

'What am I supposed to say to that?' said Eric.

'You're supposed to say the truth,' said the judge.

'It was too long a question,' said Eric. 'By the time he came to the end I'd forgotten the beginning.'

'Hear, hear,' said Mr Tewkesbury admiringly, but he said it faintly to himself.

'Mrs X didn't mention the parcel before you did, did she?'

'No.'

'Weren't you getting a bit anxious by that time that she'd forgotten it?'

'I wasn't anxious about anything.'

'Didn't you want the parcel? You'd come to get it.'

'That was up to them.'

'So, if Mrs X hadn't given it to you, you'd have just gone away?'

'Certainly.'

'And you wouldn't have told any lies to the father?'

'Probably wouldn't have seen him.'

'So you wouldn't have said anything to him at all, true or false?'

'Most likely not.'

'But, if you got the parcel, you were going – to use your own words – to head the father off?'

'Yes.'

'And the way you'd head him off would be by saying something to him?'

'Yes, I've said so.'

'So it comes to this, doesn't it? No parcel, no heading off. Parcel, and you tell the father something to head him off.'

'Something like that.'

'What did you think was in the parcel?'

Although everyone knew that the price was £50,000, it was a horrible question for Eric to have to answer. It seemed almost impossible to answer it without looking guilty, or at least self-conscious. But it had to be done. This was a question he couldn't avoid. After a short pause: '£50,000,' he said.

'Are you a rich man, Mr Smith?' asked counsel.

'Of course not,' said Eric.

'Then £50,000 must seem a lot of money to you?'

'It's quite a lot.'

'Had you 50,000 shillings of your own at the time – that's £2,500?'

'No.'

'Perhaps you had 50,000 pence. That's a little over £200.'

'Yes, I had.'

'Where had that come from? Mr and Mrs X?'

'It could have.'

'It could have come from anyone. But didn't it in fact come from them?'

'I had money of my own as well.'

'I dare say. But some of your 50,000 pence had come from Mr and Mrs X?'

'I expect so.'

'Then, wherever it had come from, only having 50,000 pence …'

'I had more than £300.'

'No doubt. How much of it from Mr and Mrs X?'

Eric regretted his interruption.

'I don't remember.'

'Well, never mind. Having under £1,000, shall we say, wasn't the prospect of getting £50,000 a very desirable one?'

'I was prepared to accept it.'

Counsel checked himself from saying that that was very magnanimous of Eric.

'So you had gone to the house to collect £50,000 in a parcel which you were prepared to accept if it was offered to you?'

'Yes.'

'And, if you got it, you'd speak to the father, and, if you didn't, you wouldn't?'

'Something of the sort.'

'Why didn't you ask Mrs X if they were still prepared to offer you £50,000?'

'There was no need.'

'Wasn't there? She said nothing about it. It was you who raised the subject with your "there was a parcel, wasn't there?"'

'I mentioned it.'

'You mentioned it because you wanted it, didn't you?'

'I didn't ask for it.'

'Why did you mention it then?'

'In case she still wanted to give it to me.'

'You seem very anxious that no one should think you made a demand. Are you?'

'That's what I'm charged with, isn't it? Demanding with menaces.'

'Not exactly,' said counsel. 'But never mind about the actual charge for the moment. You've always been anxious, haven't you, that no one should be able to say you'd demanded anything?'

'Well, I haven't.'

'Then, if you've a clear conscience on the subject, why did you ask Mr X to write that piece of paper about payment being made voluntarily and all their own idea?'

'That was the truth, wasn't it?'

'Was it? All their own idea to pay you £50,000 in return for your heading off the father?'

'It meant a good deal more than that to them,' said Eric incautiously.

'You mean the possible loss of their child meant more to them than £50,000?'

'You can't value a child in money.'

'I agree, but it was what you said I was referring to. "They valued their child at more than £50,000", I think you said.'

'They begged me to head off the father.'

'And they pressed £50,000 on you to do it?'

'Yes, they did.'

'And you were prepared to accept it?'

'Why not? If they valued my work at that amount, why shouldn't I take it?'

'You didn't think you were being overpaid?'

'A lot of people are overpaid.'

'Then you agree that you were being overpaid?'

'It isn't a crime.'

'That's a matter for his Lordship and the jury. But do you agree that you were grossly overpaid?'

'It was a lot, I agree.'

'Compared with what you had to do to earn it, it was a fantastic amount.'

'It was a lot. Some people have earned a million easier.'

'Oh – who?'

'No one in particular. I've read about such things.'

'So you thought £50,000 was a fair amount for Mr and Mrs X to pay you for your services?'

'They agreed to pay it.'

'Now let's come to the first charge against you. Threatening to publish or refrain from publishing ...'

'I didn't threaten anyone and there was never any question of publishing anything. I'm not a publisher.'

'It's lawyers' language, I'm afraid,' said counsel. 'Publishing includes speaking or writing to a person. Threatening includes saying something to a person. You don't have to produce a mask or a revolver or even an ugly look. If I said to you, "I will tell your employer what I know unless you give me £50 and I won't tell him if you do give me £50," that would be threatening to publish.'

'Is this supposed to be a legal lecture or something?'

'Well, you've got to understand the question,' said counsel. 'So I'm explaining it before I ask it. The section under which the charges are laid makes it an offence for a person to threaten to publish or refrain from publishing any matter or thing about any person whether living or dead with intent to extort any property from any other person. Now you did say that whether or not you headed off the child's father depended on whether you were paid £50,000. So you said, if you pay me £50,000 I will say something to the child's father and, if you don't, I won't.'

'What am I supposed to answer to all that?'

'The effect of your conversations with Mr and Mrs X was that, if you were paid, you'd speak to the father, and, if you weren't, you wouldn't.'

'What of it?'

'And you intended, did you not, to get £50,000 from Mr and Mrs X if you could?'

'I intended nothing. They offered it.'

'You hoped to get £50,000?'

'I hope to win the pools.'

'Quite so. Many of us do. This was almost as good as the pools, wasn't it, and you hoped you'd get the money. All I'm asking you is – you hoped to get it, didn't you? You hoped for it?'

'I may have.'

'Have you ever been in for a football pool?'

'Yes.'

'Have you ever gone in for it without hoping you'd win a big prize?'

'Of course not.'

'You wouldn't say about the pools that you "may have hoped to win a big prize"; why do you say that you *may have* hoped to get £50,000 from Mr and Mrs X? You hoped for it, didn't you? And I might add you hoped for it very much indeed, didn't you?'

'If they'd give it me, yes.'

'And you felt pretty confident, on the day you collected the parcel, that the fear of losing their baby would make Mr and Mrs X pay almost anything?'

'I didn't think about it. They offered it and I took it.'

'You mean you thought you took it,' said counsel, and sat down.

So the whole of the evidence had been given without Mary and Bill learning a word about the father. What had happened? They had pretty well been promised that the questions would be asked. Well, they would have to wait before they learned the answer. So they listened as patiently as they could to the speeches of counsel and finally the summing-up of the judge. Among other things he said this: 'Members of the jury, this is in one way a somewhat unusual case. In most trials for serious offences there is a substantial dispute between the evidence given on behalf of the prosecution and the defence. But in this case the prosecution's evidence is virtually admitted. And what you have to ask yourselves is whether what the accused did amounted to a crime. Of course, in considering that question you will pay careful attention to the evidence of the accused himself. In this country no man can normally be convicted of a serious crime, unless he intended to do something wicked. If you doubt whether the accused had any such intention, you will acquit him.

'You have heard the accused's explanation of what happened. If you have some doubt as to whether or not he was fleecing Mr and Mrs X unmercifully, playing on their love for their adopted child, you will acquit him. It is not for him to prove his innocence but for the prosecution to prove his guilt. The Crown has got to prove to your complete satisfaction that this man was deliberately squeezing Mr and Mrs X, until out of desperation they paid him. A good deal has been said by the accused and his counsel about the absence of any demand. The actual section under which the charges arise does not in fact contain the word "demand". The two important words it contains are "threaten" and "extort". To threaten, in this context, means simply to say or imply that you will do or refrain from doing something which you know the person you are speaking to will want you not to do or to do, as the case may be. To extort means to squeeze something out of a person which is not due from him and which he would not otherwise pay.

'No particular words are necessary to constitute a threat. Indeed in some cases no words at all are necessary. For example, if with one hand a man pointed a revolver at another man's wife and with the other hand made motions to indicate that he would like some money, that would amount quite plainly to a threat to shoot the wife if the husband did not pay. Similarly, if one man knew that another man did not want something about him published in the newspapers, the mere lifting of a telephone receiver, without a word spoken, could amount to a threat to publish; and, if it were accompanied by a physical indication that money was required, it would constitute the offence with which the accused is charged.

'The question you, therefore, have to ask yourselves, is: "Was this a *bona fide* piece of business, albeit with a very large sum coming the way of the accused as a result, or was the accused by his visits and by what he said at those visits plainly threatening Mr and Mrs X with some disclosure to the father of their child if they did not pay him well?" And bear in mind that it is not for the accused to prove that this was a *bona fide* piece of business; it is for the prosecution to prove to your complete satisfaction that it was not. They must prove, in other words, that all this talk about no demanding and no threats, all this talk about Mr or Mrs X offering the money and not being asked for it, is pure eyewash, and that it is a plain and simple case of brutal blackmail. They must prove that the accused terrified Mrs X with the thought of losing her child with the deliberate object of extracting money from her or her husband or both of them.

' "She offered the money", he said. "I never asked for it." You will consider first whether a loving mother might very well offer anything to avoid losing her child, and secondly whether an ordinary man like the accused would not know this. If you think it possible, even faintly possible, that when the accused started his chats with Mrs X he had no guilty intention of any kind, that he was just a friendly man exchanging a few words over the garden gate with a little boy and his charming mother and that, as far as the accused was concerned, he was immensely surprised at being offered money, even the fantastic sum which he eventually came to collect, then you will acquit him.

'Members of the jury, the law is sometimes said to be an ass, and undoubtedly there is no system of law either here or abroad which does not contain serious flaws. But, as far as these offences are concerned, you need not worry about deficiencies in the law. The word "blackmail" does not occur in the Statute book. The various offences which are commonly called blackmail are couched in various terms. One of them is called "demanding with menaces". There are more words in the section than those, but that is not the section under which the accused is charged, and those words are enough for my purpose. Do you think the accused was aware – if only vaguely – that "demanding with menaces" could be an offence? Is that why he made his statement to the police when he was stopped with the parcel, and why he asked Mr X to write on the piece of paper which was found on him when arrested? Be that as it may, in this case all you have in effect to consider, members of the jury, is whether this is a plain case of blackmail, as plain as you can have, or whether there is some doubt about it. If there is any doubt about it, you will acquit the accused; but, if not, you will convict him. There are four similar charges against him. I personally cannot see any reason for differentiating between them. If you convict or acquit on one, in my opinion you should convict or acquit on all. Perhaps you would like to retire.'

The jury retired but returned in ten minutes with a verdict of guilty. It was then disclosed that Eric had several previous convictions for comparatively trivial crimes and had been sent to prison on two occasions. Mary and Bill then learned why prosecuting counsel had not persisted with his questions about Hugh's father.

'My Lord,' said counsel, 'my learned friend told me in the middle of my cross-examination that the accused had met this child's father in prison. Accordingly I did not proceed with my questions, lest the fact that the accused had been to prison might become known to the jury.'

'Very proper,' said the judge.

'There is one matter, however,' went on counsel, 'which I should like to mention to your Lordship. As you may imagine, both Mr and Mrs X have suffered the greatest distress as a result of the accused's behaviour. They are now left in a state of complete uncertainty. Has the accused ever met the father? Does the father intend to take steps to try to set aside the adoption order and so on? Naturally, no question has been asked of the accused since his arrest on these matters. It occurs to me, however, that he could in a very slight way atone for the distress he has caused Mr and Mrs X, by giving this information now.'

'I see,' said the judge. 'I shall postpone sentence on the accused until next Session. He has heard what you have said and can act upon it or not as he and his advisers think fit. It would not, however, be fair of me to allow this to happen without saying that I consider this to be one of the worst cases of blackmail which it has been my misfortune to hear and that, in my opinion, the maximum sentence for each of the offences with which the accused is charged is far too little for this particular case.'

CHAPTER TWELVE

Mr Tewkesbury's Good Advice

For Bill and Mary the possibility that Hugh was the son of a man serving a prison sentence was a great shock. What Eric had said was not necessarily true, but the way in which the statement had come to be made had the semblance of truth. Nor could they think of any reason for Eric's telling his counsel that the boy's father was in prison, if it were not true. The mother had said that he was a solicitor. That could still be true. He might no longer be a solicitor or he might have been sent to prison for a motoring offence. Once again it was the not knowing which was most disturbing. The mother might have been lying altogether. The father could be a hardened criminal with a record for violence or fraud, or someone like Eric. Whatever he was, they would love Hugh none the less and want him just as much. But it was terribly worrying not to know. More particularly for Mary.

'It's environment that counts,' Bill said to her. 'Hugh's been with us ever since he was under eighteen months. There's nothing wrong with his progress.'

'But you wouldn't expect him to show criminal tendencies yet,' said Mary, always ready now to torture herself.

'He's not going to show any criminal tendencies,' said Bill, 'at any time. If he does, it'll be entirely your fault. In any event we still don't know for certain who his father is. I wonder if that fellow will talk. I'm afraid the judge gave a pretty clear indication that he'd get the maximum sentence in any event. I suppose it wouldn't be fair not to, but it's not much help to us.'

Meanwhile Eric was having a conversation on the same subject with Mr Tewkesbury.

'Why should I tell them anything?' he asked.

'My boy,' said Mr Tewkesbury, 'you've nothing to lose by doing so. And you might gain something.'

'That's likely, after what the old fool said.'

'No, not likely, but still possible. When my time comes,' Mr Tewkesbury went on, 'I'll tell them anything they want to know. I'll make it up if necessary. If it knocks off a couple of months, that's something. You won't notice it at the beginning of your sentence, but you'll notice it all right at the end. After all, if he's going to give you seven years, he could just as well say six years, nine months. You wait till the years are up and it's only a question of months. You'll be sorry then.'

'You speak as though you'd been there yourself, Mr Tewkesbury,' said Eric.

'Often,' said Mr Tewkesbury, 'in my imagination. And it's the last few months that go slowest.'

'As a matter of fact,' said Eric, 'there's very little I can tell.'

'Pooh!' said Mr Tewkesbury. 'We can soon put that right. You tell me what you do know, and I'll make up the rest. If I do it well enough, I might get you another month off.'

'You really think he'll take something off, then?'

'Quite frankly, I don't,' said Mr Tewkesbury, 'but it's not impossible. Odd he should do it in a case of blackmail. Quite normal in a case of receiving and so forth. "You say where the stuff is or who else was in it with you and I'll knock a bit off the sentence." Oh – they don't say that, of course. But that's what it comes to. But in a case of blackmail, I should have thought it might have stuck in his throat. Take a receiving case where sentence is postponed. What's the object of the postponement? To get information about the stuff. From whom? From the prisoner. As the judge said, no words have to be used. But he's saying to the prisoner as plainly as if he used the words: "If you'll say where the stuff is, I may knock something off your sentence. And per contra, if you don't, I won't." Isn't that squeezing information out of a chap, just as you squeezed money out of the Woodthorpes?'

'I didn't make a single threat.'

'Oh, really,' said Mr Tewkesbury, 'you can drop all that now. As a matter of fact, I thought you did a very neat job. But it's the old story. Too greedy. The number of clients I've had to say goodbye to just because of that. D'you know, I once had a fellow who burgled every house in the same street. I tried to stop him, but it was no use. It was too dead easy, he said. They caught him in the last house. Now I could understand it from the artistic point of view. It would be rather tempting to make a complete job of the whole street. Of course, it was only a small street. Seven houses, I think. Well, I could understand a man who'd done the six wanting to finish the picture by doing the seventh. But that wasn't his reason. It was just too easy. He might as well have been caught doing the first. Got seven years, I think. But I've a terrible memory. I shall forget what you've got within a week of your getting it.'

'You can look up the maximum sentence and deduct three months,' said Eric. 'I'll tell you all I know.'

'Good boy,' said Mr Tewkesbury.

'Well, it was interview day,' said Eric. 'My girlfriend came to see me, but we ran out of things to say. Well, there was a chap next to me seeing his wife or his girl, I didn't know which at the time. I got listening to them and I heard her say she was moving and I took a note of the address, in my mind, of course. I wrote it down later.'

'Why?'

'Well, as I'd been in the same place as her husband, I thought I might do a bit of sob stuff. And then I heard them talking about the boy. He was obviously nuts about him, kept on asking about him.'

'What was the man in for?'

'Manslaughter. A small boy. He was charged with murder but the jury said manslaughter. Ten years he got.'

'Well, what happened?'

'I came out soon afterwards and paid a call on Mrs West, she called herself. The fact that I'd been near her husband made her listen. Asked me in and we got talking. And then it happened. I asked after the boy. 'What boy?' she asked. But she'd gone white and I could tell she was lying. That put ideas into my head. I went on at her. She told me to go. I got up very politely but casually said that I should write to the man about there being no child. That shook her. "No," she said. "You mustn't." "How d'you spell mustn't?" I said. She reached for her bag. That suddenly gave me an idea. "Where is the boy?" I asked. She wouldn't tell me at first. Said she didn't know. So I got up again. She burst into tears. Eventually she admitted that she was not married to the father and that she'd had the boy adopted. I forced the address out of her.'

'I wonder how she knew it,' said Mr Tewkesbury. 'She shouldn't have. Or perhaps it wasn't a serial number.'

'What's all that in aid of?' asked Eric.

'It doesn't matter,' said Mr Tewkesbury. 'You blackmailed her into giving you the address. Two for the price of one, you might say. And that's how it all started?'

'More or less,' said Eric.

'Well,' said Mr Tewkesbury, 'I thought I'd have to fill up the picture for you, or at any rate varnish it. But I don't think it's necessary. You tell them all this, and you may live to bless me during your last year. That's, of course, if you live at all. But there's no reason why you shouldn't. I'm told the food's better than it was.'

CHAPTER THIRTEEN

More Conferences

When Mary and Bill heard what Eric had said, they were horrified, but they wanted to know more. Was West a solicitor or had he been one? What were the exact circumstances of the crime? But Eric simply did not know, except that he was able to say that he was in for ten years. The judge, indeed, before passing sentence asked Eric if he had given all the information in his possession, and he assured the judge that he had.

'Very well,' said the judge. 'I believe that you have done what you can to help and, though this is not a case which calls for the least clemency – indeed, as I said before, it is the worst case of its kind I have ever heard – nevertheless you have done something to help and that little will be reflected in my sentence. You will go to prison on each of the first three counts for two years and on the fourth count for ten months. The sentences will run consecutively. That will mean six years ten months in all.'

It was no less than Eric had expected, and he had got two months off. So he was a little grateful to Mr Tewkesbury for his advice. But, as the solicitor had said, the time for gratitude would come towards the end. A man facing a sentence of nearly seven years takes little comfort from the fact that it is not quite seven years. Eric went to the cells a sadder man, but little wiser.

Mary and Bill were glad to see him go, but not out of revenge. Neither of them was the sort of person to want revenge, except possibly for a very short time. But they were relieved that he would not trouble them any more. As for the future, they were left in a state of complete uncertainty and so they went again to Mr Luttrell and told him what had happened.

'It sounds as though he was speaking the truth,' said Mr Luttrell, 'and I can only tell you what the possibilities are on the basis that he is. If he isn't, we have absolutely no knowledge of what the truth is and it would be impossible to make the faintest guess as to what may happen. But, if what he said is true, it does mean, I'm afraid, that there is a man in prison who is unaware – unless he has since been told – that his child is no longer at the house where he left it. Now, don't be too alarmed,' he added, as he saw Mary's face pale. 'If we have been told the truth the father and mother are not married. And, if that's so, not only is the father's consent not required, but, as I think I told you before, he has no right whatever in the matter, unless he is liable under an order or agreement to pay maintenance.'

'But how can we tell whether he is or he isn't?' asked Bill. 'Should we try to find out?'

'On the whole I think not,' said Mr Luttrell. 'That might very well stir things up. In any event, it would not improve your chance of keeping the child.'

'Improve our chance,' said Mary almost desperately. 'D'you mean that we have a good chance of losing him? We can't. We won't. You must prevent it.'

'If we do nothing, we shall never know what to expect or how to prepare for it,' said Bill. 'For example, if we knew there was likely to be trouble, we could go and live abroad. We shouldn't hesitate if there were danger of losing Hugh.'

Mary looked gratefully at Bill.

'But naturally we don't want to do anything so radical unless it's absolutely necessary. It would be a complete upheaval and I'd have to consider the financial position. But if we knew that there was a real danger of our losing the boy, we'd want to make preparations. And the longer we had the better.'

'That's true,' said Mr Luttrell, 'but consider this aspect. The man will very likely never know about the child until he leaves prison. That might not be for years. The child will be nine in, say, seven years. If you then decided to go abroad, it would only have to be for about seven years. If you stir things up now the man could start proceedings now, and you might have to go abroad for twelve years. Besides, as I've told you, it's very likely that he has no rights at all. It doesn't sound as though there was an affiliation order. If there wasn't an order, why should there be an agreement? It's quite true that the agreement doesn't have to be in writing, but, if the parties were living together, why should they have made an agreement?'

'Very easy to invent,' said Bill. 'If they both said there was one, what chance would we have?'

'There's no sign whatever that the mother's interested in the matter. She parted willingly with the child and has never made a move since. She doesn't want the child obviously. In any event, you must remember that, if the worst came to the worst, and if the father could prove that there was an agreement for him to maintain the child, he is only entitled to be heard by the Court in the matter. And, when he was heard, what on earth could he say to make the Court upset the order? Here is a man who has an illegitimate child and then goes to prison. The child is in a happy home and has been for two years. What judge in his senses would take the child away from that home, whatever the father said? It would only be if the boy was his legitimate child that there could be real trouble. Then I agree that there could be. But there is no father named on the birth certificate. So the chances of the man having the rights of a legitimate father are minimal.'

'So you mean that, whatever happens, unless Hugh is legitimate, we can't lose him?' said Mary, rather more happily.

'I think I can fairly say that,' said Mr Luttrell. 'I can't see how any Court could take that child away from you, unless it had to do so. And the only circumstances in which it might have to do so would be if he were legitimate.'

'But even then,' said Bill, 'the welfare of the child would come first, surely? And, as you said, no sane man could take Hugh away from his happy home and hand him over to an ex-jailbird.'

'That isn't quite so,' said Mr Luttrell. 'The present law is that an adoption order cannot be made without the consent of both legitimate parents, unless that consent is unreasonably withheld, or unless the child has been abandoned or neglected by its parents. Now, suppose this husband – because I'm assuming for this purpose that they were married – suppose this husband, living happily with his wife and child, is suddenly taken off to prison. The wife then puts the child out for adoption. The husband knows nothing of this. He might have the right to have the order set aside, and to refuse his consent to a fresh order being made. Unless the Court held that he was being unreasonable it would have to allow his objection, even though it thought that it would be better for the boy to stay where he was.'

'We'll go abroad,' said Mary.

'Mrs Woodthorpe,' said Mr Luttrell, 'you're forgetting that this is not a husband, that is to say it is in the highest degree improbable that he is a husband. And, unless he's a husband and Hugh is his legitimate son, in my considered opinion, although it would of course be distressing for you to have fresh proceedings and to have the matter hanging over your head, there would be no real chance of your losing the child.'

'How can you be so sure he isn't a husband?' asked Mary.

'Well, Mrs Woodthorpe,' said Mr Luttrell, 'in the whole course of my career I have never yet seen a birth certificate with no father's name filled in where the child was legitimate. It stands to reason. No one would deliberately bastardise a child in that way. No sane person, anyway.'

'What about a mother who hated her husband and hated the child?' asked Mary. 'She might do it, mightn't she? She loathes her husband, she doesn't want children, she finds herself in the family way, is frightened of an abortion; it would be quite possible, wouldn't it, for her to run away, resume her maiden name and, pretend she was just another unmarried mother?'

'To gain what?'

'To revenge herself on the wretched child. There are these strange people in the world.'

'I'm surprised,' said Mr Luttrell, 'that anyone so devoted to children as you are, Mrs Woodthorpe, could even imagine the existence of such a creature. It is possible, I agree, but it's not a possibility we need consider. It's far too remote.'

'If that's right,' said Bill, 'then we've nothing to fear. The worst that can happen is that the father can make himself a bit of a nuisance, but nothing more.'

'That's my opinion,' said Mr Luttrell.

'Forgive me mentioning it again,' said Bill, 'but, before we went to court for the adoption order, we came to you, and I think you now agree that you were wrong in advising us to take a short cut. If Judge Hazlewell had dealt with the mother, probably she would have confessed the truth, the father would have been found and the whole problem dealt with then. Then there could have been no blackmail and no anxiety now.'

'That is so,' said Mr Luttrell. 'I've told you I'm sorry, but the chance was such a small one, I thought it worth taking.'

'But in fact it wasn't,' said Bill, 'as we now know. I have to make up my mind on the terribly important question whether we should go abroad or not. You've given your opinion. It was wrong the first time. May it not be wrong now?'

'Of course,' said Mr Luttrell, 'it could be wrong. We can all be wrong. And, even when we're right, a judge can say we're wrong. There is no certainty in human affairs. If you're worried about the matter, I suggest you take a further opinion. Or, if you liked, we could go to counsel about it.'

'And he might be wrong?'

'Of course. But if he confirmed my opinion you could feel that much more confident. And I take it that's one of the reasons you're consulting me now. To relieve yourselves of anxiety as far as is possible. If that's so, the more opinions that are the same as mine, the less anxiety.'

'But, if they weren't the same as yours, the more anxiety?'

'That's true.'

'What would you do in my place, Mr Luttrell?'

'Nothing.'

'You wouldn't go abroad?'

'Shouldn't dream of it.'

'Well,' said Bill, 'my wife and I will talk it over and let you know if we want any more help. Thank you for seeing us.'

On the way home from the solicitor, Mary and Bill both thought to themselves for a bit. Bill spoke first: 'Darling, I'll do whatever you want, but personally I think he's right.'

'I certainly don't want to uproot ourselves if it isn't necessary and, apart from that, it wouldn't be fair to you.'

'Don't worry about that. Everything's fair to me that I want. All I want is for you to be happy, you and Hugh.'

'What about his suggestion of getting another opinion?'

'More legal waffle if you ask me. "On the one hand there is this. On the other hand there is that. My opinion is this, unless the judge may think something else. On the whole the risk is small but, of course, there is a risk. Not a large one. If the father turns up, nothing will happen. At least probably not. Of course it might. One can never be sure." And so on, and so on. I'm getting quite good at it myself.'

'You are,' said Mary. 'That might have been Mr Luttrell. I wish we could go and ask Judge Hazlewell himself. He seems to be the only man worth considering. I suppose that's impossible?'

'Quite impossible, I should imagine. Certainly old Luttrell wouldn't hear of it. We might just call on the old boy. Then he'd fling us out. But that wouldn't do us any harm. A bit undignified. I wonder if I know anyone who knows him. Let me think. Tony Briar would certainly know someone who did. No harm in asking.'

Anthony Briar was a middle-aged QC who had been a friend of Bill and Mary for many years. A cheerful bachelor, he lived in the Temple by himself. Cooked for himself, cleaned for himself, and at the same time conducted a large practice. If he was ever depressed, he did that by himself too. No one ever saw him otherwise than as a carefree, jovial man. The sort of man who, on losing a leg in an accident, would have congratulated himself on not losing both. Or, if killed in an accident in summer, would, on reaching the other world, have said it was a bad summer and high time to move on. Or, if in winter, that he was lucky not to have missed the cricket.

Although a formidable opponent in court, he hated keeping to the point in general conversation.

'Well, well,' he said, when Mary and Bill told him of their experiences and fears. 'I read about the case but had no idea you were Mr and Mrs X. I expect I was the only person who didn't know. This X and Y business is quite right, but it's far from leak-proof. What an experience! And poor Mary! Now it's over, though, don't you find it interesting to have met a blackmailer? I would. The only criminal I've ever met took one of my two bottles of milk. I gave him the other, poor fellow. Must be hard put to it to steal milk. But blackmail. That's nasty, really nasty. Can't imagine wanting to share a cabin with a blackmailer, what!'

'We didn't find it at all funny,' said Bill. 'Mary nearly went out of her mind.'

Tony took her hand and patted it.

'I can well believe it,' he said. 'Poor dear. But it's all right now as far as he's concerned. Like being mauled by a lion and then hauled away to safety and the lion shot. An interesting experience once it's over. I find everything interesting. Even when my barber poured boiling water over my head. It was so hot I thought it was cold and kept my head there an extra second.'

'What did you call him, Tony?' asked Bill. 'Surely you were angry then?'

111

'I expect I should have been, if it had been done on purpose.'

'You ought to drive a car,' said Bill. 'That would soon get the anger glands going. Even you would get cross when a chap selfishly cut in front of you.'

'I expect so,' said Tony, 'an excellent reason for not driving a car. I don't want to learn to get cross. True, it would be a new experience, but I'm sure I'm better without it. But you're here to talk about yourselves, not me. What can I do?'

They asked him tentatively if he could get them an interview with Judge Hazlewell.

'He's a judge of the same Court as the judge who made the order. I'm afraid not, old boy. It's quite true that, if the case came up again, he'd refuse to have anything to do with it, if he'd advised you as a friend. But it wouldn't be satisfactory for you to see him. One can't be too careful about these things. There'd be no question whatever of justice being tampered with, but it might look as though it had been, which is almost as bad. Suppose you did have a chat with him and later the father brought proceedings in that court, and Bramcote decided them in your favour – why shouldn't the father think that the thing had been fixed between the two judges, that is if he knew of your visit? It wouldn't have been true, but you couldn't really blame the father for thinking it, could you? You do see that, don't you?'

'Yes, I do,' they each said.

'What I could do,' went on Tony, 'would be to introduce you to another County court judge miles out of London, say, and ask for his opinion. But quite frankly I really don't think it would be of much value. Every judge is different. You've seen for yourselves the different approaches of Bramcote and Hazlewell. And, you know, I wouldn't say the one was right and the other was wrong. Bramcote's been sitting for many years and I don't suppose any of his cases have gone wrong before or will again. Half the people who've appeared before Hazlewell, or at any rate a good number, have quite unnecessarily, as it turned out, had to wait an extra month or more before they got the order they were yearning for. Personally I prefer the Hazlewell technique. I like to be as sure as possible. But, for your one case where Bramcote's methods came adrift, there must be many hundred people blessing him for not giving them an extra period of waiting.'

'Yes, I see that,' said Bill. 'But we want to know two things. First, is there anything we should do now? Secondly, what are the chances of anything going wrong?'

Tony thought for a little time.

'I can't see what you can do now. It's obvious that it's in the boy's interests that he should stay with you. You have no duty towards the father. Certainly no legal duty. Morally, I suppose it might be said that as you have learned that he may possibly – only possibly, mind you – have been deprived of his legal rights, you should inform the Court that made this order, and suggest that it gets in touch with him. From the practical point of view that would have the advantage of bringing things to a head. You would then learn fairly soon if the father had any rights and if he wanted to exercise those rights.'

'It might put ideas into his head,' said Bill.

'There is that. But I don't see why he should want to make a nuisance of himself. Unless, of course, he saw money in it like our friend Mr Smith. After all, he is a criminal. Or he might just be bloody-minded.'

'But, if what Smith said is true, he sounded terribly fond of his son,' said Mary. 'If it's true that the woman gave

113

Hugh away without his knowing anything about it, it will be awful for him. And not his fault.'

'He shouldn't have gone to prison,' said Tony. 'None of this would have happened if he hadn't been convicted of some crime. So you owe your happiness to a man going to prison.'

'Don't,' said Mary.

'I wasn't being serious,' said Tony. 'If you'd never had Hugh, you'd never have been anxious about him. If you'd had another child, it might have developed measles and gone blind. If you hadn't been born, you wouldn't know anything about it anyway. I can trace my existence to a lift being out of order. My mother had to walk up the stairs and she met my father coming down them. She slipped and he picked her up. And here I am. If the lift had worked, where would I be now? Where would you be? Not here, anyway. But, to get back to the point, I should leave things well alone, if I were you. I think your solicitor was quite right. Do nothing, say nothing, wait for the call of the gentleman – to quote that strange telegram of Sir William Waterlow, while the fraud on the Bank of Portugal was taking place with Sir William's innocent assistance. Expensive assistance. It cost Waterlows I don't know how much. But this is rather a long way from your troubles. No, if I were you, I'd do nothing, and I shall be very surprised indeed if anything untoward happens. You can't forget it, of course not. That's impossible. But relax, as far as possible. And remember, time is on your side. And as each week, each month, each year goes by, you'll feel safer and safer and safer. And you will be. And, I can say this. No judge is going to take Hugh away from you, unless he's absolutely got to. And however much sympathy there may be for the father, I don't think that any judge would give him back the child now.'

114

'Then,' said Mary, 'you can say quite definitely that Hugh is ours for ever?'

'If I weren't a lawyer, I certainly could. But, when one doesn't know the facts for certain, it's impossible to give an opinion for certain. For example, suppose the father's name was left out of the birth certificate by the mother although he was the legitimate father, things might be different. But I can't believe for one moment that that happened. I could invent other possibilities to torture you with, but I won't. The fact is that it is in the highest degree improbable that anything will happen. You'll have to be content with that. But I personally wouldn't lose any sleep over it.'

'You'd never lose any sleep over anything,' said Bill.

'I nearly got married once. That kept me awake, I can tell you. But I got to sleep just in time.'

CHAPTER FOURTEEN

The Other Side of the Picture

Mary had to be content with this advice, which seemed to be very good. As the months went by she gradually ceased to worry. Occasionally she had a terrible nightmare, but she was soon comforted, when she woke up, by the sure knowledge that Hugh was in the next room. And what a wonderful boy he was, even though his father may have been an abnormal criminal. Life became as happy for Mary and Bill as it was immediately after the adoption order had been made.

All this time Hugh's real father, Randolph West, was in prison waiting as patiently as he could for the great day of his release to arrive, when, as he fondly thought, he would be reunited with Hugh. The one thing that had kept him relatively sane during his imprisonment was his love for his son. Fathers vary. Some, like Bill, are fond of their sons and will do all in their power to help them, but do not have the intense love of a woman for her child. But some fathers are very like women in their deep devotion to their children. Randolph West was a father of this kind, and from the moment he started to serve his sentence he concentrated on his son.

At first he lived on his memories. He had not been in England when the child was born, and it was not until after he had seen the child on his return, a month after the child's birth, that he suddenly realised that he loved the mother and adored the child. Over and over again he thought about all that happened during Hugh's first year. Even the most trivial events. The first smile that was not a smile but only wind, and the first real smile. The teeth that never seemed to come and the ones that appeared as if by magic overnight. How he had gloated at first because Hugh spoke to him before his mother, until he was told that da-da is the first childish sound and would be used by a child equally to a gorilla as to its father and mother. The inoculations and vaccination. Hugh was wonderful with them all. One year. Yes, so much happened. Over and over again he thought about it. He asked for a book from the prison library. It was Dr Spock's *Baby and Child Care*. It was not much in demand in prison.

After a time he began to think of the future and to watch Hugh grow up at a distance. Here Dr Spock was most helpful and enabled him to visualise what might be happening to his little son. Sometimes he took fright as a result of something which he read, and he wrote to the mother as soon as he could, begging her to take care. To provide for this and to avoid that. And in no circumstances to be afraid to call the doctor.

It was odd that a putative father should be so fond of his son. But the father was not as putative as the mother had made out to the adoption society. It was true that they had met at a dance, and that Hugh was on the way shortly after the national anthem had been played. But, from a month after Hugh's birth, they had lived together and become fond of each other. It was the wrong way round but that wouldn't have mattered so much if they had been able to marry. Unfortunately Randolph was already married. His wife had left him, whether for another man he did not know for certain. But she had only been apart from him for under a year when Hugh was born, so that a divorce was impossible at the time. But Randolph and Margaret intended to marry as soon as they could.

Margaret Parton, Hugh's mother, was twenty-seven when she had met Randolph at the dance. He had attracted her physically, as she had attracted him, but it was only after the baby's birth that a firm attachment had begun to develop. Randolph paid for all the expenses of Hugh's birth, but he did not start to live with Margaret until after he had been born. He had come back from a business trip and went at once to see the two of them.

It took him quite by surprise. As soon as he saw them both together, his whole outlook changed. This was his son. But not just his. Margaret must share the credit. After his first unsuccessful, childless marriage, he had not considered the possibility of ever having a home and a family. Then suddenly he was a family. Margaret and Hugh and he. A completely new sensation surged through him. Stout Cortez may have had much the same feeling when he stared at the Pacific. It was a new world and he realised it within a minute.

Fearfully he had picked up the baby and looked at it tenderly. He said nothing and then handed it back to Margaret. She smiled at him, but nothing was said for a full five minutes. Then he said: 'I want to come and live with you, if I shan't be in the way.'

'Darling,' she said, and kissed him.

'He's wonderful,' said Randolph. 'Why haven't we done this before?'

'Well,' said Margaret, 'you can't say we wasted any time. When will you come?'

'I'm here,' he said. 'I'm staying, if I may.'

They had eleven happy months together. They were beginning to look forward to the day when they could get married and they decided to wait till then before Hugh was christened. And then came the tragedy when Randolph was arrested and charged with murder.

He had given a lift to a small boy whom he had found walking alone on a main road and taken him to the local police station. A week later the boy had been found sexually assaulted and dead. By what were, according to Randolph, a series of horrible coincidences but, according to the police, natural links in the chain of evidence, it looked as though Randolph was the man. The matter was clinched when a few strands of material which could only have come from the boy's underclothing were proved to have been found on Randolph's coat. Everything else he could explain by coincidence, but not the strands. He said that he had only met the boy once when he gave him a lift. On that occasion it was physically impossible for any of the strands to have got on to his car. His only explanation was that either the laboratory technicians or the police had framed him. There was absolutely no reason why they should do this. The jury were puzzled by the case. They were impressed by Randolph's denials, but they could not get over the strands and they did not believe that the police would frame Randolph. He was a perfectly respectable man and the policemen concerned had never met him before. Having regard to the way death took place, the judge just left it open to the jury to bring in a verdict of manslaughter, and this they did. It was a compromise verdict, some of the jury not being prepared to find Randolph guilty of murder. The judge sentenced him to ten years' imprisonment. He appealed from the verdict but with no success.

Margaret despaired. She tried to believe in Randolph's innocence and always told him that she did. But deep down inside her she had a dreadful fear that he was guilty. Juries do not like convicting respectable people of grave crimes and they acquit if they can. He made a good impression in the witness box. Yet they convicted him. At the least he might be guilty. At the worst he was. While she was with him, she assured him so apparently wholeheartedly of her belief in him that she almost convinced herself. But, as soon as she left him, those dreadful gnawing doubts returned. And then other things came into her mind. His passionate love for his son. There was no doubt of this. But might it not be the product of a warped mind, which from time to time could not control pure physical passion? There was no doubt of his gentleness with Hugh when they were together. But that, she had read, was quite possible with a man who might murder another boy. Besides Hugh was under two when he was arrested. Randolph was a schizophrenic, perhaps. At times his dear, dear self and at others a raving lunatic. What was she to do?

Even if he were innocent, he would remain in prison for nearly seven years and, when he came out, he would be a disgraced man looking for some kind of job. He had been an important man in the business world. Who would want to be associated with him now? Even those who might possibly believe in his innocence would be afraid of what other people would think. And how could he live socially? Mothers would clutch their children in fear of him, if they knew who he was.

And what about Hugh? He would go to school while Randolph was in prison.

'What's your father do?'

'Well, at the moment he's doing ten years.' What an outlook! And then, when he came out, Hugh would be about the age of the boy who was murdered. Could she bear to leave them alone together? Randolph's love for Hugh was genuine beyond question. It was the great thing in his life. But who can account for the ways of maniacs? And how could anyone tell whether he was one or not?

And then another thought crossed her mind. When Hugh eventually learned the truth about his father, what would he feel? Would he believe in his innocence or be ashamed of him? No one could tell. But, whether or not Hugh could be persuaded to believe in his father, the outlook for them was a ghastly one, if not actually dangerous.

She thought about her problem for many torturing days. She, too, dearly loved her son, but in the end she made up her mind. She must put Hugh out for adoption. It was a terrible decision for her to make, but she had to consider Hugh first. It was the only thing to do. Once she had made the decision she moved to another neighbourhood, resumed her maiden name (she had been living with Randolph as Mrs West), and took Hugh to the adoption society.

It was not altogether surprising that, to cover her emotion, she affected an air of indifference which produced the secretary's remark about not treating the place as a cloakroom. She knew that Randolph would never consent and so she lied about his identity and their relationship. She was surprised how easy it was. From the way in which the story of her dance with a solicitor was accepted from the beginning she wondered if a lot of little bastards were not the sons of dancing solicitors. She said that the father was a solicitor so as to attract as good a home as possible for Hugh. She felt sure that to some extent adoption societies sent children to appropriate homes. She was told the sort of people Mary and Bill were, and was pleased with what she was told.

It was terrible to part with the boy but she felt sure that she must let him go. She already owed him enough for having him at all when she was unmarried, but to impose this extra burden on him seemed to her so grossly unfair that she would have been ashamed of herself for the rest of her life if she allowed him to bear it.

She tried to console herself by imagining how dreadful it would have been not only for Hugh but for her too if she had kept him. After she had consented to the adoption order she kept on saying to herself, 'I know I'm doing right. I know I'm doing right.'

And, when she knew that the order was actually made, she walked for miles in the streets hardly seeing or hearing anything, but looking straight in front of her. Every now and then she said aloud, 'It must have been right. It must have been right.'

Margaret now had the problem of dealing with Randolph. She had made up her mind not to tell him until almost the last possible moment. She knew how he adored Hugh and that life in prison, difficult enough as it was, would become insupportable if he knew that Hugh was gone. She replied to his letters by telling fairly simple lies. She made an excuse for not bringing Hugh to see him on her first visit, but on the second visit she told Randolph that she felt that the child shouldn't be brought into the prison. He was over a year old, was starting to talk quite a lot and who knows what might be stirred up in his memory, however unconsciously? To Randolph's argument that the boy would have to know some time, she replied that they'd deal with that problem when it arose. Meanwhile, she said, it would not be good for a child, as it grew from one upwards to be making regular visits to its father in prison. It would have to stop soon. Better not to start. Eventually Randolph reluctantly agreed.

But it seemed that, the less the father saw of the son, the more he thought about him. His letters were almost entirely about Hugh. And Margaret had to reply. She found it very difficult at first, inventing things which she thought would please Randolph. And then he started to use Dr Spock.

'I hope you don't let Hugh crawl round the kitchen while you're cooking,' he wrote. 'He might get burned from a spluttering frying pan, or you might trip and spill something on him. Dr Spock is very strong on this.'

'Don't worry,' she answered. 'I'm very careful about that sort of thing.'

Sometimes she actually felt as though Hugh were with her, as she wrote about him to Randolph.

As time went on it was plain that Randolph was working right through Dr Spock. So Margaret bought a copy too. From then on she was able to keep up with Randolph, and they each wrote long and (to Margaret) heart-rending letters about the child that, as far as they were concerned, no longer existed.

The boy grew and grew, spoke more and more, and became a real person. Margaret had to invent his likes and dislikes, his toys, his appetite, his progress generally. Randolph read Margaret's news avidly. And then, when she saw him on visiting days, he asked question after question about his son. At first Margaret had been a little embarrassed at these interviews, but soon she hardly felt she was telling a lie. The phantom world in which Hugh lived and grew seemed almost real to her.

'D'you know,' she would say, 'the other day he used a most extraordinary word. For a boy of his age, I mean. He must have heard me use it or something. He actually said that a picture I showed him was embarrassing. Can you believe it? Embarrassing! What'll he say next, I wonder?'

Randolph laughed.

'You'll have to be careful what you say,' he said, 'or he may come out with worse than that.'

'I'll be careful,' said Margaret. 'Oh – and another thing, he made you a daisy chain. And one for me too. It didn't last long enough for me to bring to show you.'

The most difficult problem Margaret had was with photographs. At first she made excuses but that could not go on indefinitely. Eventually she found a child of about the right age that lived near them, and took photographs of it. For a long time they were taken from such an angle that the face could not be clearly seen. Then very cleverly she gradually introduced bad photographs with the face blurred, until eventually Randolph became accustomed to the look of the child. Finally she risked better photographs, and it worked.

'I don't know whether he's more like you, or me,' said Randolph once. 'What d'you think, darling?'

'There's nothing in it,' said Margaret. 'He's got your eyes and my nose. Heaven knows where his hair comes from.'

For nearly two years this terrible game went on. Hugh was now three and had settled down very happily with Mary and Bill. Although Randolph was not due for release for about five years, Margaret now began to wonder how and when to tell the truth to him. It would be an appalling moment. She was fond of him but she was frightened too. Sometimes she thought of the details which she had given him about Hugh. What would his reaction be when he learned of the calculated deception practised on him? Would he go mad and kill himself? Or would he kill her first? She knew that Randolph was not normally an ill-tempered person. But who could say what such a shock would produce in the quietest of men? For seven years he would have been living with the one great hope uppermost in his mind; no, not just uppermost, filling almost his entire mind. First it must have been: how is my son? And then as the months and years went by: I shall see my son in four years. In three. In two. In one. Very soon we shall be together again. And the last year would go so slowly. With days painfully ticked off. And then would come the night before. No sleep for him that night. Tomorrow I shall see my son. Tomorrow. Life will begin again. At that stage he would probably not think so much of the difficulties. Of the fact that the boy would not know him by sight. But he would. Margaret would have kept his photograph constantly before the boy and spoken of him too. No, he wouldn't be at all a stranger. And the boy to him would be as if they'd never been parted. All the hardship of the past years would disappear. He would be with his son.

When Margaret started thinking on these lines – and she knew that there was no exaggeration about it – she sometimes grew desperately afraid. Had she been right to feed him with Hugh during all these years? Was it fair? And yet, if she had not done so, prison would have been quite intolerable.

She had confided in no one. Then one day she decided that she must talk to someone or burst. She had a job as secretary with a firm of solicitors, and was on good terms with one of the junior partners. He was unmarried and becoming fond of her. She knew that she shouldn't have let him. When he had first taken her out to dinner and had looked at her ring finger, he had said, 'You've never been married?'

'What an odd question.'

'Well, I know, you're Miss Parton. But some girls who've divorced their husbands go back to their maiden name.'

'No,' she said, 'I haven't divorced my husband.'

'Then you are married?' he asked.

She had hesitated for a moment. A woman can see three moves ahead, while a man is still wondering about the first. Three moves ahead? She often sees the lot. Right up to the first check. Sometimes up to checkmate. She knew that this young man could become fond of her. She liked him and, while she had every intention of joining up with Randolph when he came out of prison, it was a great temptation to a young woman to have someone to be fond of while she was alone.

'No, I'm not married.' And then she felt she must add, 'Not exactly.'

'Oh,' he said, and there was an uncomfortable silence. 'Forgive me,' he went on, 'I know it's not my business, but why don't you marry him?'

She could have told him that he was right, it was not his business. But in a way it was. It was perfectly reasonable for a young man to want to know where he stood before becoming associated with a young woman. And anyway he was much too nice to snub.

'He's not available at the moment.'

'I see. A divorce going on?'

'Not at present.'

'Hasn't done the three years yet, I suppose?' he said.

'Only two,' said Margaret.

'Oh well,' said the young man, 'if you don't mind going out to dinner with me in the circumstances, I hope you'll come again. I'm not married and never have been.'

So she had started going out with Jeremy Norton. And he was kind and gentle and understanding. Not the sort of solicitor who slips away with you after the national anthem and disappears. She realised that he was falling in love with her, but she was much too weak to send him away. The burden of Hugh and Randolph was so great that she needed this outlet. She knew it was unfair and that, when Randolph came out of prison, the young man would be left with only her grateful thanks. But he was grown up. He was a lawyer. One must have something in life except a burden. His heart would get whole again. You can be utterly miserable for a time in youth when the loved one goes off with someone else, but it takes two to make love, and a heart that has not been loved cannot be broken. So she told herself. Meanwhile Jeremy provided her only source of happiness while Randolph was away.

And then after two years, when thoughts of Randolph coming out started to weigh on her, she felt she must tell Jeremy. She must have help from someone. And she was lucky in her choice. The best type of human love is everything St Paul said it is. And in Jeremy's case it was full of kindness, compassion and unselfishness.

'I want your help,' she began, on the evening she told him.

'Of course,' he said. 'Anything. Anything at all. You know.'

'I know,' she said, 'and I oughtn't to ask you. You of all people. When I'm going to hurt you beyond measure. But I need help so terribly.'

'There's nothing I wouldn't do for you.'

'That's what makes me feel so awful.'

'Tell me.'

Eventually, after false starts and pauses, she told him. As she did so, he looked at her with such compassion that she had to ask him not to.

'I can't stand it,' she said. 'You're so good and kind.'

He looked away.

'I'm sorry,' he said. 'I know I oughtn't to be so fond of you. But I'm so glad I am. So happy. All I want to do now is to help.'

She took his hand and pressed it.

After a little she said: 'What should I do? What can I do? To tell him now would be terrible. To tell him later may be worse. I just don't know. I could really kill myself to get out of it all.'

'You mustn't think of it.'

'I won't. I promise,' she said. 'But d'you know why not?'

'Well?'

'It'll sound awfully silly. And in some ways I think it's dreadful of me. But d'you know ...'

She paused so long that he said: 'Go on. Tell me.'

'It's just ridiculous. It isn't really me. It's another part of me. But ... but ... I want to know how it ends.'

He smiled.

'Isn't that terrible?' she said. 'This awful problem. The dreadful shock Randolph is going to have. It might drive him mad. Anything might happen. And yet something in me – something quite outside myself – wants to know what is going to happen.'

'A lot of people live for just that reason,' said Jeremy. 'They don't like going out in the middle. It's quite natural. Man's such an inquisitive animal. Almost from the time he's born.'

'I know all about that,' said Mary, smiling slightly. 'Dr Spock has a lot about it.'

He laughed.

'It would be funny if it wasn't tragic,' he said. 'Both of you doing your homework like that.'

'I can even laugh sometimes,' she said. 'When I see what page he's got to and decide which bit I shall use next. I've actually laughed out loud, and then cried almost louder.'

'We're so inquisitive that we can't bother about the things we know about, as long as there's something else to explore. Hunger, misery and distress are commonplace. No need to investigate them. Spend millions of pounds on getting to the moon instead. Much more exciting than feeding or clothing people. That's old hat.'

'How right you are,' she said. 'You're such a wonderful man.'

'Not in the least,' he said. 'And there are, of course, two sides to the question. On the face of it, it does look pretty dreadful trying to get to the moon while people are dying of hunger and disease. But, on the other hand, in the course of getting to the moon they may learn unspeakable methods of blotting out half the earth. So long as both sides know how to blot out the other, there's a chance neither will try but, if only one side knows, it could successfully say: "Stand and deliver". So there you are. Going to the moon may be part of the race for survival. But I'm sorry. This is nothing to do with your problem.'

'But it's nice to think that there are bigger problems than mine. I'm not important.'

'Everyone's important,' he said. 'And you're very important to me. Now, let me think.'

He thought for several minutes.

'I can only think of one solution,' he said, 'and I can't pretend I think very much of it, but it may be best. I agree that you can't stop now. If a man is going to have a serious operation, the surgeon will try to do it in the most favourable circumstances. In some cases they'll wait for a few weeks to get the patient into the best possible state of health. In other words, they want him to undergo the shock to the system in optimum conditions. Well now, no one could say that a man who received a shock like this in prison would be receiving it in optimum conditions. At least, when he's out of prison, he'll have you to comfort him, you to talk to. In prison he'll probably have no one. I think you were absolutely right to do what you did. I don't think he should be told until he's actually released.'

'But where? At the prison gate? On the way home? And how? How could I actually get the words out?'

He did not answer at once.

Then: 'I'll tell you what,' he said. 'I would meet him if you liked, and tell him.'

'You?' she said.

'Yes. It would be quite easy for me. Or certainly easier for me than for you.'

'D'you think I ought to let you?'

'Why not? It'd probably be better for him to be told by a complete stranger. He'd be compelled to control himself more. Why not let me?'

'It won't be for more than five years. Will we still know each other then?'

'That's up to you. I shall always want to know you. And you're quite happy in the office, aren't you?'

'Oh – very. But it's so unfair to you.'

'Nonsense. How can it be unfair if I want it that way? You simply don't know how happy I am just to be with you. There's a limited amount of happiness in the world for most of us. It's wonderful to have found this much. And it's all due to you. Whatever happens, I shall always have you to thank.'

'It's the other way round,' said Margaret. 'You've meant so much to me. And helped me so much. And, now that you know everything, there's a weight lifted off me that you simply can't imagine. The relief is quite fantastic. I don't know how I've managed up till now. If I'd known what it would have done for me, I'd have told you months ago. Aren't I selfish?'

'It's never selfish to share things; happiness or misery,' he said. 'I want to give you the one and take away the other.'

'You have already helped me so much. It just doesn't seem possible. I shall always be so grateful. It won't be half so difficult now making up all those stories about Hugh. Now I've got you to share it with. Oh, thank you, thank you.'

But, while they were talking, Randolph was having the happiest night he had had in prison. Wide awake, but happy.

CHAPTER FIFTEEN

Good News

That morning the governor had sent for him. The post of prison governor is not one which, on the face of it appears particularly cheerful. But the governor of Randolph's prison was a particularly cheerful man, firm but sympathetic, and with a gay sense of humour.

'Ah, West,' he said, when Randolph had been brought in, 'are you doing anything particular tomorrow?'

Randolph gaped. It wasn't possible. But he liked the governor and he couldn't believe that such a man would indulge in flippancy at a prisoner's expense. It must mean ... it must mean ... but he'd had no warning of it ... he mustn't take things for granted ... how stupid of him ... he was going to be asked to get up another theatrical show ... what a fool to think of anything else. All this in less than a second.

'No, sir,' he said, 'nothing particular.' He hesitated and then: 'Just a few odd jobs,' he couldn't resist saying.

The governor looked at him sharply for a moment, and then smiled.

'I've good news for you,' he said. 'Very good news. Almost the best possible, in fact.'

Then he was right. Theatrical show! God! This was wonderful. And he'd be seeing Hugh perhaps tomorrow.

He felt a lump in his throat and hoped he'd have got rid of it before he had to speak.

The governor mercifully went on speaking.

'Tomorrow,' he said, 'I shall have the great pleasure of letting you out on parole.'

The lump remained. The governor, who had been proposing to wait for Randolph to say something, saw what the position was and went on.

'I'm not a person,' he said, 'who believes in raising people's hopes for nothing. In my view it's very wrong to let a man think that he may be released and then have to tell him later that he isn't going to be. I'll tell you what's happened. For some months now the Home Office has been looking into your trial. One of the policemen in your case was charged a little time ago with planting evidence. Eventually he made a full confession in that case – and in yours. He was convinced that you were guilty, his own little boy had once been frightened by a man, and he was determined that you should not get away with it. So he planted the strands on your coat. Ten minutes ago I had it on the telephone. I have no doubt that you will in due course receive a free pardon. But these things take a few days. I can't let you out till tomorrow, as I've heard nothing officially. But I wouldn't tell you this, unless I were quite certain that it will be official. Tomorrow morning I will be authorised to release you on parole. And I hope that within a very short time you will receive a free pardon.'

Randolph still could not speak.

'I can't tell you how pleased I am,' continued the governor, prepared to go on with his solo for a considerable time, if necessary. 'I don't often have this sort of pleasure. I congratulate you. Now there are one or two things to do and I shall want to know your wishes. You are so far the only person to have been informed. Do you wish anyone else to be told? Do you want to be met at the prison, and, if so, by whom? You're not married, but I am naturally aware of the position. Would you like Miss Parton to be told at once, or what? I dare say you'd like to think things over. It must be a shock. And even a pleasant shock takes it out of a chap. It would me, I can tell you. Now, what about it? Anyone else to be told? Or d'you want to walk in and surprise them?'

Randolph eventually found his voice.

'Thank you, sir, very much,' he said. 'And thank you for telling me so soon. There can't be any mistake, I suppose?'

'I wouldn't have taken a chance on that,' said the governor. 'No, I spoke to the Permanent Secretary myself, and he assures me that it's only a question of routine and documents now. Officer, let Mr West have a chair.'

It would have been a shame, the governor had thought, if Randolph had fainted, fallen and broken his neck. And he certainly looked as though he could have done the first. The use of the 'Mr' had an electrifying effect on the prison officer. He rushed to a chair and placed it behind Randolph.

'Thank you,' said Randolph to the warder. 'Thank you, sir,' he added to the governor.

'Oh, no,' repeated the governor, 'I wouldn't have sent for you and told you what I have, if there'd been the least doubt of it. Now, as regards telling other people, I can't do anything about that until I get the written authority. Technically it's not yet official and the Press mustn't get hold of it before it is. You're another matter. It would have been inhuman not to tell you at once, but I repeat that I wouldn't have dreamed of doing so if there were any chance of my information being wrong.'

GOOD NEWS

'Well,' said Randolph, forcing himself to think – he
found it almost as difficult to face his sudden release as he
had found it to face his sentence two years previously –
'well, sir, I think that, as you can't tell anyone tonight, I'll
break the good news myself in the morning.'

'Very good,' said the governor. 'But if you change your
mind overnight, I'll have a messenger sent as soon as I get
my written authority.'

So Randolph indeed had a happy night. A wonderful
night. Anticipation is sometimes better than realisation.
He could think of a good many happy occasions which
had been preceded by even happier anticipation. Indeed,
sometimes the fulfilment was almost a bathos. But not in
this case. Hugh and Margaret would be his again. Hugh
first, yes, very much first. But Margaret a good second. She
had been so wonderful to him while in prison. He adored
her letters, filled with accounts of Hugh's progress. She
never missed a letter or a visit, and she seemed to watch
for every change in Hugh so that she could tell him about
it. He hadn't really been away from the boy at all. How
lucky he was to have them both. And soon he would be
able to marry her. What a wonderful wife she had been to
him in everything but name. And what a wonderful
mother. It must have been dreadful for her while he was
in prison. But he'd make it up to her now. And they
needn't be ashamed of him now. He was to have a free
pardon. What a godsend! He had worried a good deal
about the effect of his conviction and imprisonment on
Hugh. Just as Margaret had, though in his case with never
a thought of giving up the boy because of it. But all that
was past. He would not only be free but unconvicted. A
man of good character, like everyone else. He'd be a
respectable man again, able to earn his living in the
normal way. No going round looking for jobs explaining

135

about his conviction. He could hear some of the replies which he would have received: 'Very frank of you to have told me, Mr West, but I'm afraid we've nothing in your line for the moment. If you'll leave your address we'll write to you if we have anything.' Or: 'This is a highly confidential post. I assume you can supply the strictest references?' to which he could now cheerfully reply: 'I'm sure the governor of the prison where I was will give me an excellent character. I earned full remission marks.'

None of that now. People who knew him by sight might look at him now but only as a man who had been wronged, not as a wrongdoer. 'How can he have endured it?' they would say to themselves. 'How terrible for an innocent man to be in prison for two years.' They would look at him with a kind of admiration. He had endured and come through. And without making a fuss. He had done it all with dignity. He had appealed to the Court of Criminal Appeal. Once only. He had petitioned the Home Office once only. There had been no frantic addenda to his petition. He had taken all the legal courses open to him with the help of his legal advisers. He had made no impassioned protestations of innocence, no wild allegations against other people, no pleas to the Press to take up his case. He had simply said he was innocent and, when the jury said he was guilty, he had sought to prove that they were wrong. And at last he had won. And he would behave with the same dignity now. The Press would no doubt want to interview him. He would answer their questions with calm and dignity. Did he want compensation? That was a matter for his legal advisers. Nothing can compensate for imprisonment. He was going on with his life where he had left off. He would do his best to forget the past. Did he want to say anything about the policeman who had given evidence against him? Certainly not. He had never cared to revile people, even if they had done him an injury. And so on. No allegations, no protestations, no pleas. I knew I was innocent. I hoped that I should one day prove it. I am thankful that I have been able to do so. What was it like in prison? You can best learn by going there, he would say.

And now for tomorrow. He would take them by surprise. He visualised the meeting. It would be a shock, as the governor's statement was to him, but the happiness when Margaret realised that he had not escaped but was free for ever! Hugh, of course, would not know him. He would have seen his photograph, no doubt, but that was not enough for a child of his age. But Margaret had kept the boy full of the knowledge of his father who would come back to them as soon as he could. He must be careful in his first approach to the boy. He must remember that he would probably be a stranger, for all Margaret's efforts. Very gently, very gradually he would seek the boy's confidence. He must on no account be presumptuous. Children could be as forbidding as dowager duchesses of the old school. He must keep his place. It might take a week, a month or much longer, but he would be patient or the boy might be resentful of this strange man taking liberties with him. But in the end all would be well. His son would know him as he knew his son. Father and son. This is my son. My son. It really was going to happen. Then he actually fell asleep.

CHAPTER SIXTEEN

The Boy in the Garden

They called a taxi for him and at nine o'clock he was on his way home. Nothing had yet appeared in the newspapers. He felt strange and nervous. No one who has not been imprisoned can appreciate the feelings of a person newly released. The realisation that he was going to meet his fellow men on equal terms gave him a curious sensation. On the whole a happy one, but with an element of fear in it, rather like when as a small boy he was first selected to play cricket for his school. He remembered the flutters in the pit of his stomach as he walked out to bat. He was batting for the school. They had chosen him out of all those others. He was one of only eleven. He remembered with regret that he was bowled first ball. No longer the exciting flutters in the pit of his stomach. Just deep misery, misery which persisted until he made a glorious catch to win the game. The spectators had risen and cheered him wildly. He had redeemed his duck. What a wonderful tea it was afterwards! But for that catch he could not have eaten a thing; he was still numb with misery until that ball came speeding his way not more than a few inches from the ground. Somehow he had flung himself at it and held it. What a moment! And now he was going out to bat again. But he'd be more careful with his wicket this time, much more careful. He would resist the temptation to pick the boy up in his arms. He must resist it at all costs. Gently was the word. Gently.

As the taxi turned into the long road where Margaret now lived, he looked out at the houses. It was a new neighbourhood to him. Possibly he had been in it once or twice but he did not know it. When Margaret moved there she had explained to him that it seemed better to change their neighbours. She did not want their pity, she said, still less their sneers.

They were bright, clean-looking houses with gardens in the front, some of them full of flowers. Yes, it looked a happy place. He had (as he thought) seen pictures of Hugh in the street. At first there was more street than Hugh but, once Margaret found that the deception had worked, there was much more Hugh than street. All the same the place did seem in a way familiar to him from the photographs. Suddenly he banged at the front window of the cab and shouted to the driver: 'Stop.'

He was very angry with himself for losing control for the moment.

'I'm sorry,' he added quietly, 'I've just seen my son. So I'll get out here and take my case. So sorry to have given you a shock. But, you see, I haven't seen him for two years.'

'OK, guv,' said the driver. 'Good luck.'

'Thanks,' said Randolph.

He took his case, paid and grossly overtipped the driver and was about to leave the taxi when the driver stopped him.

'That's too much, guv,' he said. 'Thanks all the same,' and he handed him back the whole of the tip.

Randolph thought of saying: 'I've had a free pardon. I'm not just a released criminal,' but decided on the whole to leave things as they were.

'That's very good of you,' he said. He held out his hand and shook the driver's.

'Thanks,' he said.

'That's OK, guv,' said the driver. 'Cheerio.'

And he drove off.

Randolph walked back slowly to the garden where he had seen the boy. Margaret hadn't written about the friend or friends he must be playing with down the road. 'Oh, of course,' he said to himself, 'how stupid of me. Margaret's out at work and she must leave Hugh here.'

He stopped for a moment. He hoped the boy hadn't heard the shout. He must be more careful. Here he was, determined to be quiet and controlled, and, the first moment he sees his son, he gives a great yell and hammers on the window, almost as though he were out of his mind. This must be a lesson to him. He started to walk very slowly to the garden where the boy was. He reached it and looked over the low fence. The boy was sitting by himself. A teddy bear lay beside him.

'Hullo, young man,' said Randolph, in as ordinary a voice as he could manage, but it trembled slightly.

The boy looked up.

'Hullo,' he said.

'May I come in?' asked Randolph.

The boy did not answer.

'May I?' repeated Randolph.

Still no answer.

Randolph opened the gate quietly and went slowly into the garden. The boy looked at him curiously, but did not appear frightened.

'Well,' said Randolph, 'who d'you think I am?'

The boy continued to stare.

Randolph waited a full three minutes, looking at the boy, who sat there quietly looking back at him at first. Then he turned over and pulled his bear closer to him.

'Don't bite me, bearie,' he said, and hugged it.

Eventually Randolph decided on action, and rang the bell. After a short while the door was opened by a pleasant-looking woman dressed for housework.

'Good morning?' she said questioningly.

'How d'you do?' said Randolph. 'It's very good of you to look after Hugh while Margaret's at work.'

'I beg your pardon?' said the woman.

'I'm sure Margaret's most grateful and so am I. But, now I'm back, I don't suppose it'll be necessary. Not so often, anyway. But it *has* been good of you.'

The woman looked at him for a moment or two and then said, 'I'm awfully sorry, but I haven't the faintest idea what you're talking about.'

Randolph looked at the boy again. There could be no mistake. There was no doubt whatever. He had the photographs with him. He laughed.

'I expect you're surprised to see me. For the moment I thought I must have made a mistake. But that's Hugh all right.'

'Who are you?' asked the woman.

'How stupid of me,' said Randolph. 'Of course you wouldn't know. I'm Hugh's father. Do forgive me for being so stupid.'

This is what happens to a man when he comes out of prison, he told himself. He's not used to meeting ordinary people in an ordinary way. I must be frightfully awkward. Just imagine walking into a strange woman's house and not saying at once who he was.

'Yes, I'm the guilty party,' he added, trying to find confidence in facetiousness. 'D'you think Hugh's like me?'

'Who on earth is Hugh?' asked the woman.

For a moment Randolph wondered whether the boy had wandered into a strange garden. But the woman could see the boy and did not seem in the least surprised at his presence. But perhaps she thought they'd come in together. That must be it. What an ass he was. Of course that was it.

'Stupid of me,' he said. 'I do apologise. I thought you must have looked after Hugh while Margaret's at work. He oughtn't to wander about like this. It's dangerous.'

He must really speak to Margaret about it. Was Hugh really allowed to wander about the street? It must be the people who looked after him. Margaret couldn't possibly know. Well, he'd soon put a stop to that.

'I suppose you don't happen to know who's supposed to be looking after him while Margaret's at work?' he asked.

'Looking after whom?'

'Hugh, of course.'

'Who is Hugh?'

'Let me introduce you. I'm afraid I don't know your name ...'

'Watson.'

'Hugh, this is Mrs Watson. Mrs Watson, this is Hugh.' His first introduction of his son. He'd done it the wrong way round!

'I'm sorry,' he went on. 'Mrs Watson, this is Hugh. Hugh, this is Mrs Watson.'

Mrs Watson imagined she must be dealing with a tame lunatic, at least she hoped he was tame. Better to humour him, anyway.

'And, if he's Hugh, who are you, may I ask?'

'I'm Hugh's father. I've only just come back.'

'May I ask where from?'

'Well,' said Randolph, 'that doesn't matter. The point is I'm back.'

Escaped from an asylum obviously, thought Mrs Watson. I must get on to the police. Make an excuse for going inside.

'Forgive me,' she said. 'I want to speak to my husband before he goes off to work.'

Her husband had left the house some time before, but she felt it was as well to let the stranger think that there was a man in the house.

'Of course,' said Randolph. 'I'll talk to Hugh.'

A sudden fear took hold of the woman. Lunatics, however quiet they seemed, might suddenly do anything. Kidnap the boy or even kill him. She'd take no chances.

'Come along, Georgie,' she said to the child. 'Come in with mummy.'

'Want to play with bearie,' said the boy.

'You can play with bearie inside,' said Mrs Watson. 'Come along, now. Don't keep mummy waiting.'

Reluctantly the boy got up, still holding his bear, and walked into the house. Mrs Watson shut the door.

Randolph waited, puzzled. What an odd woman. And Hugh hadn't been wandering around. This was obviously the place where Margaret left him. And the woman called him Georgie and herself Mummy. People sometimes called children by different names, but Mummy! And to shut the door on him seemed rather odd. And asking all those questions. But of course, he thought, I'm not married to Margaret. She can't have the faintest idea who I am. I might be a kidnapper or a lunatic or something. How could she tell I was Hugh's father? Stupid of me. I should have produced the photographs. He could soon put that right. He rang the bell. Nothing happened. He rang again. Still no result. He listened and could hear talking going on, but not what was said. It's all very odd, he thought. But anyway I'm back, and Hugh is only a few yards away. Probably it was silly of me to try to surprise them. Ridiculous. Of course Margaret will be at work. But not for much longer now that he was back. No more finding places for Hugh to be while she was out. A mother ought to be with her child, if possible. Dr Spock said that a child needs individual care up to the age of three. Much better that that care should come from the mother. Well, it would in future. The important period was from one to three, but he felt sure that Margaret had done the best that could be done in the circumstances. Her letters showed that. He rang the bell again. There was still no answer. It was all very odd. A few minutes later a police car arrived. Two policemen got out and came into the garden.

'Good morning, sir,' one of them said.

'Good morning,' said Randolph, and was surprised at his lack of fear. A policeman was now his friend, no longer his jailer.

'D'you live here, sir?' asked the officer.

'No,' said Randolph.

'Then may I ask your business here?'

'Certainly,' said Randolph. 'I've called for my son.'

'Your son?'

'Yes.'

'We've just been telephoned by the lady of the house to say that it's her son.'

'Her son!' said Randolph incredulously. 'I suppose she's playing some sort of game. But personally I'm getting a bit tired of it. Look, officer …'

Randolph got out his pocket book and took out some of the photographs. 'Look at these,' he said.

Both officers looked at the photographs.

'They don't tell us much without seeing the boy,' the first officer said.

'Have a look at him,' said Randolph. 'He's inside.' The officers looked at each other and then one of them rang the bell. Before the door was opened, Mrs Watson looked out of a window to see who it was. Seeing the police, she went to the door and opened it at once. The boy was with her. The officer looked at the photographs and then at the boy. There was no doubt about it. They were the same. Neither of them said anything for the moment. They just looked at the photographs, then at the boy, and then at the photographs again.

'It's him all right,' said one to the other.

This is a rum do all right, they said to themselves. We're called here about a lunatic, but which is it? Eventually one of them spoke.

'Mrs Watson?' he asked.

'That's me,' said Mrs Watson.

'Do you say the child is your son, madam?'

'Of course I do. Why on earth d'you have to ask me?'

'Well, this gentleman has a lot of photographs of him and he says it's his son.'

'Nonsense,' said Mrs Watson. 'Let me see.'

They handed her the photographs. She looked at them and was surprised at first. Then she relaxed.

'Of course,' she said. 'I can explain now. Though I don't know who this gentleman is. There's a Mrs West up the road who asked if she might take photographs of Georgie. I didn't mind. So she's been taking them ever since.'

Randolph went white, but managed to speak.

'I am Randolph West,' he said.

And then with horror he realised what must have happened. Hugh had died and Margaret daren't tell him while he was in prison. So she had pretended that he was alive and taken the photographs of another child of the same age. Yes, he remembered now. It all fitted in. He had complained that the first photographs really showed nothing of the child, and then that they were badly taken. The wrong light, the camera must have moved, over-developed, under-developed, and so on. It was only later that good photographs started to appear. Oh God! Hugh was dead. His son dead. But poor Margaret. How she must have suffered! How terrible for her to have to bear this burden alone! Well, she would have him to help her now. But who was to help him? His son. The one thought that had made his time in prison possible. And he was dead!

The policeman saw how Randolph had changed and put out a hand to steady him.

'Are you all right, sir?' he asked.

'Yes,' said Randolph drearily, 'I'm all right. I'm sorry to have caused all this trouble. I've been away, and my son – my son is dead.'

He walked through the gate and along the street. Mrs Watson and the police officers stayed chatting together.

One word ran through Randolph's mind as he walked. Dead. Dead. For some time his mind was so numb with the shock that it could do nothing else but reiterate 'dead'. But after a time some feeling returned and he tried to think when Hugh must have died. He soon realised that it must have been very early in his imprisonment. When he had the first bad photographs. But what did it matter when he died? He was dead. Where was he buried? He visualised the pathetic tiny grave. What had Margaret put on it? What did it matter? Hugh was dead. The little person whom he had left with his smiling mouth and bright eyes, his chuckles and his tears, was dead. Why? What was the cause of death? Could it have been prevented? What did that matter? It had not been prevented. Hugh was dead. The gradual coming together of father and son which he had so often visualised in his cell would never happen, never at any rate until he was dead too. He could not even wish that he were. His mind was incapable of wishing. Incapable of anything. It was as dead as a living mind in a sane and living person can be.

CHAPTER SEVENTEEN

The Lawyers Prepare

Margaret was in Jeremy Norton's room at the office when she heard of Randolph's release. He had turned on the news, and she listened to the announcement with a mixture of fear and pleasure.

'What can I do?' she asked. 'He'll probably be at home by now, waiting for me. I'm surprised he hasn't rung me here to know where Hugh is.'

'I'll come along with you, if you like,' replied Jeremy.

'No, I'll have to do it myself now,' she said. 'There's no alternative. But I can't think what will happen. D'you think I could possibly leave now? I must get it over. Until it is, I couldn't do anything properly here.'

'Of course,' said Jeremy. 'Go off straight away. And take tomorrow off too, if you want it. If you get a chance, perhaps you'd phone me to tell me what happened. I do want to know. And in any event, if you want any kind of help, you've only to say.'

'You are kind,' she said.

Within five minutes she was on her way home, wondering how she could break the news. She knew what his first question would be: 'Where's Hugh?' She would have to parry it and kiss him and say she wanted to talk to him. He'd realise from her tone of voice that something

was wrong and that might help to break the shock. Poor
Randolph. She felt infinite pity for him. Would he hate her
for it? He must. She had put out of his reach the one thing
on earth which he had lived for. From his point of view it
must seem a merciless crime. She took a taxi home. He
was in the sitting room, heard the taxi door bang, and
guessed that it was Margaret. He had been sitting in an
armchair, staring blankly at the carpet. But he must make
an effort for Margaret's sake. He was standing by the door
when she arrived. She could see from the look in his face
that something was terribly wrong. But he couldn't know
yet.

He took her in his arms and kissed her. Then he held
her away from him and looked at her.

'It's good to be back,' he said, 'but – oh, my darling ...'
and he broke off.

'D'you know?' she asked incredulously.

He nodded, then took her in his arms again.

'Oh, God!' he said. 'Why did it have to be?'

'How did you find out?' she asked.

'Mrs Watson told me.'

'Mrs Watson!! She doesn't know.'

'I mean I realised from what she told me.'

'I see.'

But how, thought Margaret, could he have guessed from
anything which Mrs Watson had said?

'Darling,' he said, 'I don't want to make things worse for
you – but I must know where he is – where he is buried.'

'Buried?' said Margaret. 'Who d'you mean?'

'Hugh, of course. Why do you ask?'

'Come and sit down,' said Margaret, and led him to a
couch where they sat together, for some time in silence.

'Randolph dearest,' said Margaret, 'I want you to prepare
for a shock.'

149

'There is nothing left to shock me.'

'There is,' said Margaret. 'Hugh is not dead.'

He jumped to his feet.

'Not dead?' he said excitedly, but, seeing Margaret's face, he realised that it was not good news which she had to tell.

'In a home? A hospital? Crippled? Can he recognise you? I must see him, whatever state he's in. Is it the mind or the body, or both? Tell me, tell me. I must know.'

'As far as I know Hugh is alive and happy and well.'

'Then where is he? What are you saying? I don't understand. Everyone seems mad today. Mrs Watson down the road, and now you. What are you telling me?'

'He's been adopted.'

'Adopted? But they can't do that. Just because I was sent to prison, they can't take the child away. You were able to look after Hugh. What are you telling me? You couldn't have consented?'

'I did consent.'

'You consented? You couldn't have. It's impossible. You loved him as I did. You wrote to me about him. Oh – God! Those photographs. Your letters. All lies. But why, my darling, why? I don't understand. Where is he, and why did you do it?'

She explained as best she could. He understood better than she had expected. From time to time he could not help saying: 'Oh, darling, why did you do it? Why did you?' And then he began to ask questions about the adopters, which Margaret could not answer. All at once he said: 'But could they do this without my consent?'

'They told me at the adoption society that, as we weren't married, your consent wasn't necessary.'

'But I'd lived with the child for a year. Surely that makes a difference?'

150

'I didn't tell them that, I'm afraid,' said Margaret. 'I was so anxious to get it over with the least possible fuss that I said I'd only met you once at a dance and didn't know who you were, except that you were a solicitor.'

'And they just accepted all you said?'

'They'd no reason to disbelieve me. That's why I moved, of course, to be out of the neighbourhood where we'd lived. In case the truth might have come out.'

'I'm going to take legal advice,' said Randolph. 'I'm not giving up without a struggle.'

'But would it be good for Hugh to come back to us after two years?'

'He's ours. I want him. I need him desperately. You can't think what I've been through waiting and waiting in prison. It was Hugh who kept me going. If it's humanly possible, I must get him back. I believe I'd almost *take* him back.'

'You'd only lose him again, and probably go to prison. For something you *had* done this time. And think of Hugh being bashed about like a tennis ball.'

'Yes, I see that,' said Randolph. 'No, I wouldn't really take him. But I'm going to see if we can get him back legally. I'm sure he'd settle down with us again after a month or two. After all, he was with us for his first twelve months. That must make a difference.'

'Why not come and see Jeremy Norton? He's been wonderfully kind to me, and I know he'd do anything to help.'

'Who's he?'

Margaret blushed slightly.

'He's a partner in the solicitors I work for.' She paused for a moment.

'And he's been so kind to me.'

'A boyfriend?' he asked.

'Sort of,' she said.

'Why not?' he replied. 'You couldn't be expected to go into a nunnery while I was away.'

She kissed him.

'You do understand,' she said. 'Let's go and see him.'

So next morning they kept an appointment with Jeremy in his office. The first thing he wanted to see were the papers which had been served on Margaret. She had kept them and brought them with her to the interview. He looked at them and then he said, 'That's odd.'

'What's odd?' asked Randolph.

'Oh – nothing,' said Jeremy. 'Just a technical matter. Now, tell me,' he went on, 'all three of you lived together for just on a year?'

'Yes.'

'And who paid the household expenses?'

'I did,' said Randolph, 'naturally.'

'So in effect you were living like husband and wife, the husband keeping the family?'

'Exactly.'

'The only difference being that you weren't actually married?'

'Yes.'

'Well,' said Jeremy after a little thought, 'it seems to me that it can be argued that there was an agreement by you to maintain the child. Such an agreement doesn't have to be in writing. Agreements can be made by conduct. They are, every day. For example, if you go into a shop and pick up an article and hand the assistant the price without either of you saying a word, there's an agreement by the one of you to buy and the other to sell the article. If you park your car on a piece of private land which has "Parking 2/6 an hour" on it, you agree to pay 2/6 for every hour by leaving your car there. In the same way by keeping the child week after week it can be said that there was what lawyers would call an implied agreement by you to keep the child, if only temporarily. All the law requires is that there should be an agreement by you to maintain the child. It doesn't even say for how long. One of you hasn't to say solemnly to the other: "Do you agree to maintain this child?" and the other answer "Yes" to make an agreement. If you both intended that Mr West should maintain the child indefinitely and he actually did so for a year, in my view there's ample material for the Court to say that there was an agreement under which you were liable to support the child.'

'Where does all this lead to?' asked Randolph.

'Well, if I'm right about that, and I can't guarantee that I am – I think we should get counsel's opinion on the matter – but if he confirms my view it seems that Mr West was entitled to be served with the proceedings and to be heard by the Court before an order was made.'

'But how could they serve him,' asked Margaret, 'if they didn't know of his existence?'

'Well, at least they could have tried a bit harder to find out. But whether they could or could not have found him, the fact remains that you weren't served and, if I'm right about the agreement part of it, you were entitled to be served.'

'Was my consent necessary, then?'

'No, it wasn't.'

'Then what difference would my being served have made?'

'You would have been entitled to go before the judge and object to an order being made. He could, of course, have refused to give effect to your objection. In many cases – in most cases – a putative father wouldn't have any chance of stopping an adoption. But a case like yours is different. You might have been living together for ten years, for example. In such a case unquestionably a judge might take a good deal of notice of what a putative father had to say. And there's a further strong point in your favour. You intended to marry Miss Parton, if and when you got a divorce.'

'I still do.'

'Fine. Well, if you marry, that will make Hugh legitimate. Now, supposing you'd gone before the judge and told him all that two years ago, he might – I don't say he would – but he might have refused an adoption order. Of course, a good deal would have depended on what arrangements could have been made to look after the child. A child of one needs a mother very badly. You'd have been asked what you could do about that. If Miss Parton had assented to the adoption, and didn't change her mind, it might have been very difficult, if not impossible, for you to satisfy the judge that an order shouldn't be made, but you had the right to argue about it. But then, I suppose, it's possible that, if Miss Parton had known – and, of course, she would have known – that you were going to the Court to object, she might have withdrawn her consent.'

'I certainly would have,' said Margaret.

'Well, if you had, I don't see how a judge could have made the order. So, if Mr West had been served, the probability is that an order would never have been made. But, even if it could have been made, Mr West lost the chance of being heard on the matter. And, in my view, if he was liable to support the child under an agreement, I believe he may have a right to have the order set aside. That doesn't necessarily mean that you'll get Hugh back.'

'Then what's the point of it all?' asked Randolph.

'It means that you'd have a reasonable chance of getting him back. And that would be something, wouldn't it?'

'It would indeed,' said Randolph. 'But what would it depend on?'

'A good many things,' said Jeremy. 'But, first of all, let's find out if my view about an agreement is right. And there's another thing we want to get on with. That's your divorce. You're now in a position to obtain one. So the sooner you do so the better. There'll be no problem about the evidence. She's never offered to return to you?'

'Never.'

'And then we shouldn't have to wait the extra year?'

'If you agree, then, I'll do two things. I'll fix up a conference with counsel to see if my view's correct and to talk over the matter generally, and I'll get him to settle the petition against your wife.'

Margaret and Randolph left Jeremy in a much happier frame of mind than when they arrived at his office. In the meantime Hugh was paddling happily in a pool in the Woodthorpes' garden, while Mary and Bill were watching him equally happily. They had not yet heard the announcement of Randolph's release. Hugh had now been with them two years and was a cheerful and promising three-year-old.

It was only in the evening that Bill heard about Randolph's release. Eric had only given his name as West, and there might have been more than one West in prison, but he felt sure it was Hugh's father. So he had to tell Mary. She was horrified and he tried to calm her.

'We can't be certain it's the same man,' he said.

'But you think it is.'

'I can't help thinking it is, but it may not be.'

'When will we know?'

'It's impossible to say. And anyway we don't know that, if he's the man, he'll try to do anything about it. But I promise you this. If any attempt is made to take Hugh from us we'll go abroad at once and I'll sell up everything.'

'You are good to me,' she said.

'But I'd hate to lose Hugh.'

'So you would, darling. You'd hate to lose him. But I'd die without him. I love you, darling, but I can't live without Hugh. I mean I couldn't live if someone took him away from us. It would be different if he died. I'd be heartbroken but it couldn't be avoided. But I couldn't live, knowing he was alive somewhere else and couldn't be with us.'

'Well, you won't have to,' said Bill. 'Very likely we'll hear nothing more about it. But, if we do, then we'll be off and away.'

'Thank God for you,' said Mary.

On the way home from Jeremy, Margaret very tentatively mentioned a subject which had been troubling her. She was devoted to Randolph and wanted to try to make up to him for the two terrible years in prison but, at the back of her mind, she was intensely worried about Hugh. He had now had two years with another family. What effect would a change at the age of three have on him? She had read and listened to comprehensible and less comprehensible pronouncements by psychiatrists on the effect of lack of security on a child. Might not another change damage the child? How she wished that she had not yielded to her overwhelming feeling that she must give Hugh away when Randolph was sent to prison. She was not in the least conscience-stricken. She still felt that what she had done was right. Of course, if she had known what was going to happen, she wouldn't have dreamed of doing it. But how could she know? The jury had found him guilty, the judge had sentenced him, the Appeal Court had dismissed his appeal, and the Home Secretary had refused to interfere. Randolph had still assured her of his innocence, but how could such an assurance prevail against all the forces of the law? And, even if she had fully believed in him, the fact would have remained that he would have served seven years in prison and been known for the rest of his life as a criminal or ex-criminal.

But, although she did not reproach herself, she expected Randolph to reproach her. It was only natural. From his point of view she must have let him down horribly. What a terrible thing to do to a man, and then to follow it up by the other lies. But Randolph was incredibly understanding and, although at first he did say twice: 'Oh, Margaret, how could you?' he soon ceased to complain of her at all. He concentrated entirely on getting Hugh back.

'You are sure,' began Margaret, 'you are sure that it'll be all right for Hugh for us to get him back?'

'All right?' he said. 'We're his parents. We made him. He has our bodies and minds in him and no one else's. Of course he'll be a bit unhappy at first, and feel strange with us. But we had him for a year. That's only two years ago. He'll soon be ours in every sense.'

'It'll be rather awful for the other people.'

'I know,' said Randolph. 'It was more than rather awful for me in prison, but I had to stand it. And, after all, they can get another. This isn't their child. They chose it like you might choose an animal. Oh – I know it isn't the same thing after you've got it, but in the first instance they couldn't have any love for a child whom they'd never seen before. And they ought to have tried to find me before they took it.'

'That was my fault,' said Margaret. 'I lied about you. So how could they tell?'

'I see that,' said Randolph, 'and it will be hard on them. But it would be harder still on me. I've been robbed of two years of my life. It can't be right that I should be robbed of my son as well.'

She saw that it would be hopeless to pursue the matter, and did not try again. She also felt that, after what she had done, she was hardly the right person to seek to dissuade Randolph from trying to get back the child.

The next morning Jeremy sent for her.

'I've been thinking about this case,' he said to her. 'Now, are you quite sure that you want me to try to get the boy back?'

'Absolutely,' said Margaret.

'Right,' said Jeremy. 'If you want him back, I'll get him back. You know there's nothing that I wouldn't do for you.'

'You are much too good,' she said.

'Pure self-interest,' he said. 'I'd prefer to be happy myself, but the next best thing is to see you happy. Now there's one thing we ought to do at once, just in case of accidents.'

'What's that?'

'Make the boy a ward of court.'

'What for?'

'It's only a precautionary measure, but it's just worth taking.'

'But why, and what is it?'

'Well, I know it's most unlikely, but supposing, when we've issued an application to have the adoption order set aside, the other people took fright and went abroad? I know it's rather far-fetched, but such things do happen. Once they were abroad, there'd be nothing you could do about it. If we make the child a ward of court he can't go abroad without the High Court's permission, and that would never be given until our application had been disposed of. So I'll get Mr West's authority and do it straight away.'

'But can a child be made a ward of court just like that?'

'Pretty well. All you have to do is to settle some money on the infant, it doesn't matter how little, and apply for it to be made a ward of court. From the moment you apply, the child is a ward of court. It's too simple, really. But that's the law, and I'd better get on with it – just in case.'

It was a dreadful day for Mary when she was given the terrible news. The first definite notice which she and Bill had that Randolph West was the child's father and was going to do something about it, was when they received notice that an application was being made to make him a ward of court. At first she wanted to go abroad just the same. But it was pointed out to her that, once the application was made, the child could not be taken abroad without the Court's permission, so that the result might be that, if they tried to get out of the country without permission and failed, both she and Bill might go to prison and would certainly have prejudiced their chances of keeping Hugh.

'It's so cruel,' said Mary. 'They can't take Hugh away from us now.'

'I don't suppose they will,' said Bill, 'but they've got to hear both sides first. Anyway, you remember that Tony and Luttrell both said that no judge in his senses would decide against us. I know it's dreadful to have it hanging over us, but you must try not to worry too much. It'll be all right in the end. Just as it was when that fellow blackmailed you. And, if you look too worried, Hugh will notice and then he'll be upset.'

Once having made Hugh a ward of court, Jeremy issued an application in the Court of Appeal, asking for the order to be set aside on the ground that Randolph had never been served with the proceedings and that, as he was a person who had agreed to maintain the child, he was entitled to have been served. Counsel had advised that this was the right course to take.

Judge Bramcote was told about the application.

'But this is very odd,' he said. 'How does the father know the name of the adopters? He could still have made his application, even if he hadn't, but it's very odd that he knows it.'

This was a fact which had puzzled every lawyer who had had to deal with the case. All prospective adopters have the right to ask that their cases shall be heard under a serial number, so that their names and addresses shall not be made known to the mother or father of the child. As Judge Bramcote said, this would not prevent the parents from making an application in the case because they would know the number of the case and the court in which it was brought. At any time they could make any proper application and the court, although it would not disclose the name of the adopters, would serve notice of the application upon them. Nor would the fact that the parents did not know the names of the adopters prevent them from making the child a ward of court, as the child could be identified. In Hugh's case, he would have been described as the infant formerly known as Hugh Parton, the son of Margaret Parton, born on such and such a day in respect of whom an adoption order had been made in such and such a court. Unless the adopters had gone abroad there would be no difficulty in serving them with the application. So the use of a serial number is no protection whatever against the possibility of an application to set aside an adoption order by a father who has not been served with the application for adoption when he had a right to be served with it.

But all the same it seemed very odd to Judge Bramcote that Randolph's solicitor knew the adopters' name and address. This was in fact due to one of those mistakes which are occasionally made even by the most careful people. A clerk in the County court had by mistake sent a copy of the adoption order to Margaret. This contained the name and address of Mary and Bill and it ought never to have been sent to her. It was this which enabled Eric to start blackmailing Mary. There were other ways in which he might have found out, but they would probably have entailed making a lot of enquiries, and the probability is he would have been unable to do so. Strangers would be more likely to learn of an adoption if they lived in the adopters' neighbourhood. And, if anyone in the neighbourhood happened to have a mind like Eric, he might have found out enough to act as he did. But the refined torture of blackmail is most unlikely when a serial number has been used, although it is not impossible. And, of course, mistakes are occasionally made. In any event an application to set aside an adoption order by a putative father, who has been ignored and has a right to be heard, is in no way avoided by the use of a serial number.

When Judge Bramcote heard about the mistake he was very angry but, beyond ensuring that the error of their ways was pointed out to all those who were responsible, there was nothing he could do about it. And, indeed, being quite unaware of Eric's previous activities, he imagined that no harm in fact had been done.

'But it might have been,' he said. 'The mother might have tried to kidnap the child, if she had changed her mind too late. Too much care cannot be taken over these matters.'

The judge said this to the registrar, who was responsible for the conduct of the proceedings of the court. The registrar said his little piece to the chief clerk. The chief clerk spoke strongly to the staff clerk in charge of adoptions, and the staff clerk took it out of a senior clerk, who was very angry with the junior clerk who had caused all the trouble. But the fact remained that it had happened.

Both sides now prepared for battle, but it was agreed between the solicitors that it would probably be better to start the proceedings in the County court rather than go straight to the Court of Appeal. They considered that this course might save time and expense. Judge Bramcote decided that it would be better if Judge Hazlewell heard the application.

Mr Luttrell advised Bill and Mary to employ a woman barrister.

'You think she'll understand a case like this better than a man?' said Bill.

'Partly that, but mainly because she's a very able person and as tenacious as a bulldog. Once she's got her teeth into anything she just won't let go. She's the woman for Judge Hazlewell. She has everything in a woman which he can't stand. He likes women to be feminine. He doesn't think the Bar is the profession for them at all. You may even see him wince from time to time when she makes a point in a masculine way. The result is that he will listen with relief to the man on the other side.'

'Well, surely that's to our disadvantage?' said Bill.

'On the contrary. He'll lean over backwards to be fair to us. He realises his faults and he will be on guard against being persuaded by the advocate whom he so much prefers.'

'But surely,' said Bill, 'the law oughtn't to be like this. It oughtn't to make any difference what judge you have. Each one of them should do justice.'

'Each one of them tries,' said Mr Luttrell, 'but each one is just a man like you and me under the robe and wig. That's one of the advantages of their dressing up. They look more impersonal. I know one of them who never takes his wig off in court even in the hottest weather, in case he should no longer look like a judge. He lets counsel take off theirs, though.'

'How d'you know this?'

'I met him once at a cocktail party and he told me. No, I agree that theoretically every judge should decide a case the same way. But perfect justice is impossible. When we have machines as judges they may do better, but, as long as we have men and women, they're going to be affected by the things which affect men and women. Now, if I know a judge had got a particular foible, I've got to pander to it. Get the case before another judge if I can, but, if I can't, it's no good to my client if I just ignore His Honour's well-known views. It shouldn't be the case in a perfect society but then you wouldn't need judges in a perfect society. At any rate we don't bribe judges in this country, except with words. And I would say that the oil of words is a great improvement on palm oil. Yes, Mrs Boulder is the girl for you. You'll like her. I'll fix up a conference.'

So a few days later Mary and Bill and Mr Luttrell attended Mrs Boulder's chambers in the Temple. Those who had known Dames Ethel Smyth and Madge Kendal recognised a mixture of the two in Mrs Boulder. She had a most forceful personality, she feared no one and, like Mr F's aunt, she hated fools.

'Sit you down,' she said, after being introduced, and then she looked at Mary.

'Mrs Woodthorpe,' she said, 'I recognise that these proceedings are and will be a tremendous strain for you. I've had children of my own and know all about it. But

163

you must try to control yourself. If you're going to weep in my chambers – which at the moment seems highly probable – what'll you do before the judge? Now, some people might think that was an advantage. Well, it isn't. At some stage in the case the judge may ask himself whether he is to send back the child to the home of a tearful woman, who can't control herself.'

'I haven't cried in your chambers, and I'm not going to,' said Mary rather crossly.

'That's because I'm being beastly to you,' said Mrs Boulder. 'The judge may be, and probably will be, exactly the opposite. He may even weep himself. Just think what the poor fellow's got to do. On the one side he has two admirable people who want the boy. On the other side he has two equally admirable people who want him just as much. One side is going to be broken-hearted. If the judge had by law to strike you in the face, he'd refuse to do it. He'd resign his office and let someone else do the dirty work. But he's got to do much worse than that. He's got to tear the heart out of one of you. I don't know how he can do it. If he lets you keep the child, that man who has served two years in prison will find himself robbed of his child without any fault on his part, except perhaps that he shouldn't have had it in the first instance. If the judge gives him back the child, you'll be quite desperate. Poor fellow, I say. I shouldn't like to bear his burden. I'll never be a judge for that reason. I suppose there have been judges who appeared to be able to drink their port all right after sentencing someone to death. There had to be in the old days, when death was the penalty for petty stealing. But I wouldn't have that job for the world. So, when you're feeling sorry for yourself, spare a thought for the poor old judge.'

Mary and Bill could not avoid exchanging glances.

164

'That's all right,' said Mrs Boulder. 'I wanted to stop you feeling too sorry for yourselves before we began. Now, let's get down to business. Hugh, I gather from your statement, is the perfect boy. That, if I may say so, is a pity. A perfect boy, if suddenly removed from you to a strange environment, is less likely to suffer serious harm. A difficult, highly strung, tearful young man would be much better from our point of view. Now I'm not suggesting for a moment that you should make up a case about him. Of course not. For one thing we don't do that sort of thing and for another the judge will probably see the boy and, if he's a normal cheerful boy, he's not going to burst into tears and bite the judge's little finger. But every child has faults and I want you to think about them very carefully. From the bad habits like biting nails to the worse things like sulking. I want you to try to think of him quite objectively and to make a list of all his defects, physical, mental and moral. He's old enough at three to have some of each. My children, I suppose, were like most fond mothers' children – the best in the world – but I could have recited a list of their faults. Mark you, I shouldn't have dreamed of doing so. They were quite perfect, I assure you.'

'But what good will this do?' asked Bill.

'It'll please me for one thing,' said Mrs Boulder, 'and the reason it'll please me is because, when you've done it, Mr Luttrell will take the list to a psychiatrist, preferably one who has not himself been certified. It doesn't need a psychiatrist to tell you that to remove Hugh from you now must be bad for the boy. But how bad? That's the question. And we want a man who'll make it as bad as bad can be. We want a man who thinks he really understands children and may be right. We want a man who is convinced that most neuroses can be traced back to childhood. It would be very nice if we could get a man who would be prepared to say that, if this child were taken from you now, he might conceivably go to the bad when he grows up.'

'Have you any suggestions, Mrs Boulder?' asked Mr Luttrell.

'Let me see,' said Mrs Boulder. 'There's Crestway. Bit of a paranoiac, but, unless you get him on his pet aversion, he's really quite sane. And lucid. He always speaks to you as though you were a dull pupil in the lowest form at school. That's the way I like to be spoken to when I don't understand the subject. He's excellent for most judges, though his didactic methods do rile some of them. The only danger with him would be if someone happened to hit on the subject of racing. He must have lost a flyer on a horse – once, or something. But he may be talking to you quite sanely and normally and, as I said, most lucidly, if the conversation is about psychiatry, and then somehow or other horse racing is mentioned. His whole manner changes. He snorts, rather like a horse as a matter of fact. And his eyes certainly look at you a bit like a horse which has seen a rather alarming piece of paper in the road. And then he begins. He grips you by the arm and a torrent of words comes out of his mouth so fast that he isn't always able to arrange the order properly. If that was his normal behaviour he'd be certified in a trice. But fortunately it isn't. I think he'd be good with Hazlewell. He's a judge who wants to learn. He wants to know why. Crestway will tell him. That's if he's prepared to support us. And I imagine that almost any psychiatrist would be prepared to support us.'

'Won't any of them come on behalf of the Wests?'

'Oh, indeed yes. I said that almost any would come for us. But quite a number would back up the other side. Now I don't see why anyone should mention racing in this case.

I don't see how the subject could possibly arise. Unless, of course, our opponent knew of Crestway's little foible and managed to introduce the subject. D'you know who it is?'

'Our opponent?' said Mr Luttrell. 'Not at the moment. I can ask, of course.'

'It wouldn't help really. I happen to know about Crestway because I met him once, and during a pause in our conversation I asked him if he was going to the Derby.'

Mrs Boulder held out her arm.

'I sometimes think I can still feel the bruise he made on my arm when he gripped it.'

She thought for a moment.

'I think perhaps we'll keep him in reserve. We may want two. So we'll make Crestway a reserve. It's a pity, because he's so clear in what he says. And he really thinks he's right. Most persuasive he is. This judge doesn't like psychiatrists and it's as well to have one who speaks well. But we couldn't risk him by himself. Now, who else is there? Ah – I know. Baldry. Frank Baldry. The great thing about him is that no one would ever know he was a psychiatrist. It's his stock-in-trade. He's aware of the prejudice against his profession and the jokes that are made about them. And it's plain to see that he's studied the art of being ordinary. He'd be a wonderful actor. His throw-away lines are worth listening to.'

'Throw-away lines?' queried Mary.

'Yes. You know the way an actor will sometimes say something that you can hardly hear. It's either a good joke or very important. The trouble with many actors is that they throw it away so successfully that no one can hear it. But, when they ensure that it is heard, it's a most effective method of advocacy. The sort of thing I mean is this. Suppose Baldry was being examined about a man's mind, he'll describe his findings in a very matter-of-fact tone and end up quite casually with something like: "The sort of mind, you know, you find in a murderer". But he throws away "murderer" so cleverly that, though you hear it perfectly, it sounds as though it only just reached you. It seems so casual, as it does with a good actor, but it's all most carefully studied. Yes, I think Baldry for our number one. Crestway for our reserve. Now we'd better have someone else in case of accidents. I know. Mallet. He's just the opposite of Baldry. Mallet looks and talks like a psychiatrist. He's a very little man. Rather like a bird really. What sort of bird? A chicken, I suppose, is the nearest. He'll talk quite slowly for a time and then suddenly he'll see a tempting morsel, something he really feels he knows all about, and peck, peck, peck he goes, peck, peck, peck. He's got all the degrees and he's written a book on dreams and insomnia. Should be in every hotel room, like the Gideon Bibles. He's even invented a method of preselecting your dream. It's a bit complicated and I've never found it to work. But it sent me to sleep all right.'

'I'm most grateful for all this advice,' said Mary, 'but what I want to know is whether we're going to win our case.'

'Fair enough,' said Mrs Boulder. 'My opinion is that you will.'

And then, noticing Mary's immediate pleasure, added: 'But, of course, I may be wrong. If it's any comfort to you, though, I wouldn't have said that just to make you happy. You're paying me for my opinion and you're entitled to know what I really think. And that's what I think. I think you'll win. But it'll be no use coming round after we've lost and saying "You said we'd win", because I haven't. I've given you my opinion on the facts we know. On these facts you should keep the child. But I can't guarantee that the judge will say the same and, of course, if new facts of which I know nothing emerge, obviously I can't say what the effect will be.'

'But what new facts could there be?'

'How can I tell? Something in the family history of the Wests which psychiatrists will say make it highly desirable that they should have the boy. I don't pretend that's likely but, just as I've told you to list the boy's faults, so they're being told to think of anything that might help. Frankly I can't think of anything we don't know already, but I don't know everything. Now, if there's nothing else, please prepare that list as quickly as you can, give it to Mr Luttrell and he'll get on to Baldry, Mallet and Crestway. Try to get some sleep, Mrs Woodthorpe. The hearing isn't for three weeks and you'll be in no condition to give evidence if you don't. You don't want to arrive pale and bleary-eyed. Leave that to the judge.'

Much the same sort of thing was happening to Randolph and Margaret. Jeremy had also suggested that they should brief a woman.

'Hazlewell's a bit susceptible to women,' he said, 'if they're nice-looking. I don't mean he decides in their favour when he shouldn't, but he does listen to them most attentively.'

Jeremy's advice was to brief Miss Frayling. She was a most attractive young woman of thirty-eight, married, with three children. She retained her maiden name for professional purposes. She had a particularly persuasive smile. Men witnesses sometimes found it dangerously seductive.

'Well, would you agree with me about this, Mr Plainfield?' she would say, with a smile which seemed large enough for the whole court to bask in, though it was directed solely at Mr Plainfield. And Mr Plainfield had the greatest possible difficulty in disagreeing. Indeed, it had been said of her that she had persuaded an independent witness of an accident to say that a car which he had sworn was going forward at about twenty miles an hour was in fact going backwards.

She also advised that a psychiatrist should be called, for the purpose of saying that Hugh would come to no harm if he went back to his real parents. She was particularly anxious that the divorce enquiries should be speeded up. She pointed out that, if it could be shown that an undefended divorce petition was on its way to a hearing, it would be a tremendous advantage. On Randolph and Margaret marrying, Hugh would automatically become legitimate. Indeed she had advised that a divorce petition on the ground of desertion be pressed on as quickly as possible, and that an application should be made to adjourn the hearing of the proceedings to set aside the adoption for at least six months. By that time the divorce decree would have been made absolute and Randolph and Margaret could be married. But in spite of Miss Frayling's eloquence the application was refused by Judge Hazlewell.

'It would be very wrong,' he said, in refusing it, 'to allow this matter to be postponed for any time at all unless it is essential. If the boy is to be moved back to his natural parents, the sooner the better. If he is not to be moved, the parties on both sides should not be subjected to any further suspense. It is quite true that, if the applicant were married to the mother by the time his application is heard, he would have a stronger case. But if he and Miss Parton say that they intend to marry as soon as divorce proceedings have made their marriage possible, and if they are believed when they say this, their case will be nearly as strong as if they were actually married. Not quite as strong, it is true, but very nearly. And it is to be noted that they have made this application to adjourn the matter. It is opposed – quite properly I think – by the adoptive parents but, having opposed it, it will be very difficult for their learned counsel to ask me not to believe that the natural parents intend to marry. The applicant offered him the proof of the pudding by asking for an adjournment. Having refused this offer, it will be almost impossible for him to satisfy me that it was not a genuine one.'

CHAPTER EIGHTEEN

Fathers at Lord's

.

The day before the application was due to be heard Bill spent at Lord's. Although he felt fairly confident about the result of the case, he became almost terrified at the thought of losing it. This was infinitely worse than the original application for adoption. Then they had known Hugh for only three months. Now it was two years. He was desperately afraid of the effect on Mary if they lost. On this occasion he found it much harder to be interested in the cricket. He actually failed to notice a catch at the wicket, although he was looking straight at the batsman. His thoughts were far away and it was only a loud appeal that brought him back again.

'What was that for?' he asked his neighbour.

His neighbour looked at him. 'Didn't you see?' he asked.

'As a matter of fact, I didn't,' said Bill.

'Caught at the wicket,' said his neighbour. 'No doubt whatever about it. Kellogg started to walk away almost before the appeal.'

'I'm not really very much in a mood for cricket,' said Bill. 'Shouldn't have come, really.'

'Oh, I don't know,' said the neighbour. 'Should take your mind off things. I always come here when my wife's going to have a baby. It's wonderfully peaceful.' He paused, and then went on: 'Very difficult at home. We've seven of them, all under twelve.'

They clapped the incoming batsman. Another man came and sat next to Bill. After a short time he spoke: 'I'm told you're Bill Woodthorpe.'

'That's right,' said Bill. 'Have we met before?'

'No, but I expect we shall tomorrow.'

'Good God!' said Bill. 'You're not …?'

'Yes, I am. Randolph West. I came here in the hope of finding you. Could I have a word with you over lunch?'

'About the case?'

'Of course.'

'What d'you want to say?'

'Then you'll listen?'

'I don't know that the lawyers would approve.'

'Lawyers!' said Randolph. 'You'll forgive me if I don't think much of the law. I say, well stopped.'

He clapped his hands a few times.

'This is the best fielding side I know,' he said.

'Yes,' said Bill, 'they're pretty good when they're in form. People talk about cricket as though the players didn't have to train like in other games. Have to be jolly fit to do the job properly. You can't move quickly unless your whole body and all your muscles are in trim. You can soon tell if one or two in the side have been beating up the town.'

'All the same, there've been some very fine drinkers in the game,' said Randolph. 'Can't think how they did it sometimes. D'you remember … well, he's dead now so I won't mention his name, but he'd walk on to the ground as though he'd prefer to lie down on it – and well he might after what he'd got through the night before – but, if anything came within yards of him, he was on it like a

173

panther. Wonderful chap. Pity about the drink. But I suppose he liked it. You been a member here long?'

'Ten years or so. You?'

'About the same. Well, what about it? Will you have a word?'

'If you won't tell the lawyers.'

'OK. I won't. D'you play much yourself?'

'Not now. I used to play a good bit. What about you?'

'I think I can fairly say that I'm the only member of the MCC who has played for the inmates of one of Her Majesty's prisons. I took three wickets, and made eighty.'

'Good for you. Where was that? Or shouldn't I ask?'

'D'you know, I'm not absolutely sure. I was moved about a bit. You get prison memory, you know, like people used to get Middle East memory. Though the prison kind is different. Every day goes so terribly slowly and sometimes, I know it sounds absurd, you forget where you are. It doesn't seem possible. And then, if you've changed prisons, you sometimes think you're in one when you're in the other. And dates are hopeless. Anyway, I made eighty and took three wickets. It's not in Wisden, though.'

'What is it you want to tell me?'

'Must you go through with this?'

'It's you who started it,' said Bill.

'But it's our child. Why don't you let us have him back?'

'How could we? It would pretty well kill Mary.'

'Then you wouldn't mind so much?'

'Of course I should, but men are different.'

'Not me,' said Randolph. 'If I had a million pounds, I'd offer it to you for Hugh.'

'Does he mean so much?'

'I simply can't tell you how much. I should have felt very much the same if I'd been exploring the South Pole for two years, but not quite. You've never been in prison. I suppose it's different for the regulars. But if you've never been there before, and you know you've got to wait years inside, you simply have to catch hold of something to stop yourself going mad or as near mad as doesn't matter. I caught hold of Hugh. He became my whole existence. I ate Hugh, I drank Hugh, I slept Hugh. I was Hugh. He was me. I talked aloud to him. He talked aloud to me. I had to do it softly or the other fellows got annoyed. It's bad enough to annoy the screws but far, far worse to annoy your fellow prisoners. Like at school but much, much worse. I could well understand a chap already half mad taking a wild dislike to me for talking softly to myself. Suddenly it could have come over him, not being able to get away from the soft-talking prisoner. It would become an allergy with him, and eventually he'd try to get rid of it by destroying me. They'd have called it murder. It wouldn't have been anything of the sort. He wouldn't have hated *me*, it would have been my beastly mouth working up and down and saying nothing that he couldn't bear; he would have to get rid of it, like a ticking clock or something else you can't stand. Fortunately it didn't happen, and I soon realised that I had to be careful.'

'It must have been dreadful for you. And didn't it make it worse to know you were innocent?'

'I just don't know. When all my appeals failed I almost began to think myself guilty. After all, everyone else had found me guilty. Was I the only one in step? It has a terrible cold-making effect, prison. It was cold physically too. But I don't mean that. It makes your head and heart cold, or nearly. And you can't live with a cold heart. And Hugh kept mine warm. How can you keep him from me now?'

'If it were only me,' began Bill, and then stopped.

'Well?' said Randolph.

175

'You've had the hell of a time. Oh – well hit. That was a beauty. It's a six. No, just not.'

'If it were only you?' persisted Randolph.

'Well, it isn't. You say you nearly went mad in prison. Mary might go mad if she lost Hugh.'

'I had no one in the prison to help me. Your wife has you.'

'There are limits to what a husband can do.'

'Won't you even try?'

'I couldn't possibly. You've had a very rough time and to say I'm sorry sounds trivial. I can't say I fully understand, as only someone who's been in prison could do that.'

'You're dead right.'

'But, short of that, I can visualise how appalling it must have been for you.'

'Appalling's right. And d'you know what happened when I came out? I found Hugh at the other end of our street.'

'What on earth d'you mean?'

Randolph explained.

'You can imagine what sort of a blow that was. There he was, playing in the garden. My dream had come true. Hugh and I were going to be together again. And then – when I heard about the photographs – I thought he was dead. Imagine the walk home. All the joy of freedom gone. Only black despair. And then I'm home and learn the truth. I admit it was a relief in one way. But, if I couldn't get him back, he was dead to me.'

'Isn't it something to know he's well and happy? He's a wonderful little chap.'

Randolph smiled slightly.

'He must be. I don't suppose he's anything like the other little so-and-so. D'you think he's like me at all?'

Bill looked at Randolph.

'I hadn't really looked at your features and it's a little difficult for me as a matter of fact. Mary likes to pretend he's like us. But he isn't, of course. I should say he may have got your nose. But it's a bit early to say.'

'My nose,' said Randolph. 'You haven't a photograph on you, I suppose?'

'Well, I have, as a matter of fact.'

He took out a pocket book and showed Randolph a picture of Mary and Hugh together.

'That's about a year old.'

'She looks a sweet woman, your wife, if I may say so,' said Randolph.

'Thanks. I think so.'

Randolph scrutinised the snapshot.

'It's a bit difficult, for me at the moment,' he said. 'I'm so used to the other one that this one looks like a stranger.'

'Well, if he's a stranger to you, you'll be all the more a stranger to him. He can't remember you from two years ago. Isn't that a reason for ...'

Bill broke off.

'No doubt it seems like that to you. But it isn't my fault I haven't seen him for two years.'

'I know. But what about the effect on Hugh? The doctors say it'll be bad for him.'

'Well, we've got one who'll say he'll be fine. But, between you and me, this isn't a matter for trick cyclists. It's a matter of justice. Pure justice. Can you give me any reason in justice why I shouldn't have Hugh back?'

Bill thought for a moment.

'Well, I could,' he said eventually, 'but I don't want to sound offensive or like one of your lawyers.'

'Go ahead,' said Randolph. 'After what's happened to me, a few words won't hurt.'

'Well,' said Bill, 'you weren't married to the girl. If you had been, this would never have happened.'

'Why d'you say that?' asked Randolph. 'Margaret could have lied about me just the same.'

'Oh no, she couldn't,' said Bill. 'Your name would have been on the birth certificate and your consent would have been necessary. They'd have had to look for you. And they'd have found you. You'd have refused your consent, and we should never have had Hugh at all. To that extent it's your fault.'

'I suppose your lawyers will make a lot of that?'

'They're bound to. They'll use everything they can.'

'But I paid for the child before it was born and right up to the time I was sent to prison. That's not like putting a girl in the family way and running off.'

'Of course not,' said Bill. 'That's just what I wish you had done. Then we shouldn't be where we are. You wouldn't have any rights at all.'

'I did all the things a married man would have done. All but marry the girl. And I couldn't do that. I shall as soon as I can.'

Randolph paused for a moment and then said: 'Tell me, do your lawyers say you're going to win? Don't tell me if you'd rather not.'

'Yes, they do,' said Bill. 'They think we will. What about yours?'

'They think so too.'

'Which d'you mean – think that we'll win, or you'll win?'

'That we will.'

'That's what they're paid for, I suppose,' said Bill. 'If they haven't confidence in their case, who's going to have it? Like boxers or politicians, they're always quite certain they're going to win, until they've lost. Wouldn't do to let the other side know you weren't sure. You'd start half-beaten. Good Lord, I didn't notice. They've come in for lunch. Shall we go and have a bite?'

'OK' said Randolph.

And the two fathers went off to drink beer and eat sandwiches at the Members' Bar at Lord's. Cricket is a friendly game.

CHAPTER NINETEEN

Evidence and Argument

The next day the case came on in Judge Hazlewell's private room. No one wore robes. The judge was in a lounge suit and sat at a table. Mrs Boulder and Miss Frayling sat opposite him. Their solicitors sat just behind them. Mary and Bill sat behind their solicitors and Randolph and Margaret behind theirs. At the side of the table, near to the judge, was another chair for the witnesses, and next to the witnesses' chair was a chair for the clerk. It was all rather crowded. Had not the wrong form been sent to Margaret, the parties would have been kept separate from each other. But, as they each knew each other's name and address, there was no point in this.

When everyone was ready, Miss Frayling opened the proceedings. After a few preliminary remarks saying who represented whom, she went on: 'Your Honour, this application (which by consent is made in the first instance to your Honour instead of the Court of Appeal) is to set aside the adoption order on the simple ground that my client, Mr Randolph West, had a right to be heard before the order was made and that, as he was deprived of that right, he has an absolute right to have that order set aside.'

'Isn't it a matter of discretion?' asked the judge.

'With respect, no, your Honour,' said Miss Frayling. 'It is an elementary principle of English justice that every person who has a right to be heard on any particular matter shall be given the opportunity of being heard. That was not done in this case. Indeed, I may add, nobody bothered very much about my client. They just accepted the mother's say-so that he was not to be found. If the mother had been brought to court and examined on oath, she would have had to admit that she knew exactly where the father was, that she had lived with him as a wife, and that it was not just a casual affair after a dance.'

'Be that as it may,' said the judge, 'if I set aside the order, I could still make it again after having heard the father.'

'That is so, your Honour, but …'

'It must be very rare for an adoption order to be refused when the mother consents, just because the putative father objects.'

'I agree, your Honour,' said Miss Frayling.

'Well, then,' said the judge, 'if I hear the putative father's objections, and consider that they would not have weighed with me so as to prevent an order being made in the first place, what is the point of setting aside the order?'

'I will tell your Honour quite simply,' said Miss Frayling. 'When your Honour's learned colleague, Judge Bramcote, made the order he certainly had the mother's consent. But, if your Honour were to set aside the order and a fresh application for an adoption order were made, your Honour would certainly not have her consent. I appear both for the natural father and the mother, and I can assure your Honour that the latter will withdraw her consent as soon as she gets the opportunity.'

'I see,' said the judge. 'Should that happen, I should then have to say that her consent was unreasonably withheld before I could make the order.'

'Precisely,' said Miss Frayling.

'Well, in that event,' said the judge, 'there still seems no point in taking two bites at this cherry. If you satisfy me on the evidence that in all the circumstances the child should go back to his natural parents, the application should be allowed and an adoption order refused. On the other hand if, when I've heard the whole of the evidence, I'm satisfied that the mother's consent is unreasonably refused and that the putative father's objections should not prevail, your application to set aside the order should be dismissed.'

'That, I agree, would be the effect, your Honour,' said Miss Frayling, 'but, in the event of this case going further, I wish to insist on my client's strict legal rights. And one of these is, in my submission, that, provided your Honour is satisfied he was under a legal liability to support the child, this adoption order should be set aside, whatever may happen thereafter.'

'But surely,' said the judge, 'it must be a matter of discretion, even if you are correct in saying that your client was entitled to be served and it was through no fault of his that he was not served. An adoption order affects the status of the child. For all, or nearly all, legal purposes an adopted child becomes the child of Mr and Mrs A, instead of Mr and Mrs B. All sorts of things might have occurred as the result of the changed status of the child. Grave injustice might be done to people other than your client if the order were set aside, to people who were as innocent as your client. In such cases surely the Court has an overriding discretion to decide whether the order should be set aside. I would have thought, subject to any argument of yours to the contrary, that the position would be the same as after a decree absolute of divorce. In such a case a husband or wife who has not been served may apply to have the decree rescinded, but, though the Court may rescind it, it isn't bound to do so. In such cases innocent people may be involved. The parties may have re-married, children may have been born, and so forth.'

'Well, your Honour,' said Miss Frayling, 'I see the force of your Honour's argument. Fortunately for my client nothing of the kind has happened in this case and I would respectfully submit that, if it is a matter of discretion, unless other innocent parties are affected, my client has a right that discretion should be exercised in his favour.'

'You may be right,' said the judge, 'but the child is an innocent party, is he not? And he has certainly been affected, if only by living two years with Mr and Mrs Woodthorpe.'

'There has been no further change of status, your Honour.'

'Does there have to be? The receipt of a fortune would not effect a change of legal status, but surely I should have to consider such a matter before rescinding an adoption order. The child is as innocent as your client. I should have thought that his situation was a matter relevant to the exercise of my discretion.'

'Well, your Honour,' said Miss Frayling, 'I will reserve further argument about the matter, as I hope to satisfy your Honour in any event that, if it is a matter of discretion, it should be exercised in my client's favour.'

'Very well, then,' said the judge. 'You'd better call your evidence. But, first of all, I suppose, you should limit yourself to proving your client's liability under an agreement to support the child. Because, unless you prove that, that's an end of the matter. I gather that there are some distinguished medical gentlemen here. There's no point in their time being wasted in giving evidence if the application is to fail anyway.'

'I agree, your Honour,' said Miss Frayling, 'so I'll call Mr West straightaway.'

Randolph took the oath and sat in the witness chair. In answer to Miss Frayling he said he had paid for the expense of Hugh's birth, that he was abroad when the child was born but that, on returning to the country two months after the birth, he and Margaret had lived together as husband and wife until he went to prison. He had paid for the child's maintenance from birth.

'I take it,' said Mrs Boulder, cross-examining, 'that no affiliation order has ever been made against you, Mr West?'

'It wasn't necessary,' said Randolph.

'You simply kept the mother and child?'

'Exactly.'

'Supposing you'd ceased to keep the mother – I'm not referring to the child for the moment – could she have sued you for failing to do so?'

'That would be for my lawyers to answer.'

'As far as you know, were you liable to the mother under any kind of agreement to support her?'

'Not as far as I know.'

'Now, coming to the child,' said Mrs Boulder, 'your case is that you were liable under an agreement to support the child?'

'Yes.'

'But you only supported the child in the same way as you supported the mother?'

'I suppose so.'

'Nothing was said about your being liable to do so, or anything like that?'

'No, except once, in fun, she said she could get an order against me.'

'She didn't mean it?'

184

'I'm sure she didn't intend to go to court about it. We were lovers, and she said it laughingly.'

'Quite so. Now your case is that you were liable under an agreement to support the child. What agreement?'

'An agreement by my conduct in continuing to support the child.'

'We're very legal, aren't we?' said Mrs Boulder. 'Hardly the language of a layman, is it?'

'Is that a question to the witness, Mrs Boulder?' asked the judge.

Mrs Boulder looked at the judge.

'I stand rebuked, your Honour,' she said. 'But this conduct of yours, Mr West,' she went on, 'was no different from your conduct in keeping the mother.'

'There was this difference,' said Randolph. 'If I'd failed to keep her, she couldn't have sued me but, if I'd failed to keep the child, she could have taken me to the police court and got an affiliation order against me.'

'I wonder you need to have a lawyer to appear for you at all, you know so much about it,' said Mrs Boulder, almost to herself. 'Forgive me, your Honour,' she added, 'but I almost felt it was Mr West's solicitor answering, or was it my learned friend Miss Frayling?'

'I don't see why I should forgive you twice for the same offence within half a minute, but I will,' said the judge.

'Thank you, your Honour. That is all I wish to ask,' said Mrs Boulder.

'Mr West,' said Miss Frayling in re-examination. 'Will you tell his Honour a little more about this occasion when Miss Parton, or should I say Mrs West, said she could get an order against you?'

'It's a little embarrassing,' said Randolph.

'I'm afraid you'll have to overcome your embarrassment,' said Miss Frayling. 'Your answers might be important.'

'Well,' said Randolph, 'we were in bed one night and we were teasing each other. She had done something to me, I'm not sure what, pulled my nose, or pinched me or something, and I called her a little bastard. I'm afraid, your Honour, that lovers do sometimes use language like that to each other, and even worse, purely in fun.'

'I dare say,' said the judge who, sitting so close to the parties and undistinguished by wig or gown, had difficulty in not showing slight embarrassment. His wife and he were very happily married. 'I dare say,' he repeated. 'Go on, please.'

'Well, when I called her that, she said: "Not so much of your little bastard, or I'll be taking you to court about yours." '

'Very well,' said the judge. 'What happened then?'

'Nothing, your Honour,' said Randolph. 'I mean, nothing more was said on the subject.'

'Thank you, Mr West,' said Miss Frayling. 'Now, I have Mrs West here who can corroborate Mr West on this part of the case, but I don't think it's really in dispute. The question is whether an agreement by conduct has been proved. But, if my learned friend wants to cross-examine Mrs West on this aspect of the case, I'll call her at once. I shall, of course, be calling her later, if your Honour decides this point in my favour.'

Mrs Boulder indicated that she did not want to cross-examine Margaret on the point, and proceeded to address the judge.

'I suggest, your Honour,' she said, 'that no agreement has been proved. It is true that Miss Parton, I beg your pardon, Mrs West, could have gone to the Magistrates' court if Mr West had ceased to support the child, but could she have sued him in the County court? In some cases the regular payment of money will establish a legal relationship, such as rent or payment for work done. But why should a payment by one lover to another create any legal relationship? I do not use the term "lover" offensively. I would say the same if they were husband and wife. A husband is normally bound to support his wife, and if he doesn't, she can make an application for maintenance in the Courts. But that doesn't mean that if he's been regularly giving her, say, £30 a week for maintenance and suddenly stops, she can sue him under an agreement to pay £30 a week, unless they had made a binding agreement to this effect. And happily married people or people happily living together don't make such agreements – they don't need to.'

'But, Mrs Boulder,' said the judge, 'if the true facts about this child and its mother and father had been brought to the notice of the Court, Mr West would undoubtedly have been made a party to the case, wouldn't he?'

'Yes, your Honour, I agree,' said Mrs Boulder, 'but only because the Court would have said that he was a person who ought to be heard on the matter, not because he was liable under an agreement to support the child. As your Honour knows, the court has power to make any person it thinks proper a party to adoption proceedings. And I make a present of the fact to my learned friend that, if your Honour had known the true facts in this case, you wouldn't have troubled your head as to whether Mr West was liable under an agreement; you would have said, "whether or not he is liable under an agreement to support the child, he ought to be made a party to the proceedings." But, until your Honour said that, he had no right to be served with the proceedings, and neither your

Honour nor Judge Bramcote said that, and the order was duly made. Consequently, although it may be hard on Mr West, the fact that he would have been made a party to the proceedings if the true facts had been known, is irrelevant to this application, unless he had a right to be served with them. And he only had that right if either he was liable under an agreement to support the child or if the court had ordered him to be joined in the proceedings. In my respectful submission, neither of these conditions was fulfilled and this application should be dismissed.'

'Your Honour,' said Miss Frayling in reply, 'lovers and husbands and wives who are living happily together don't normally sign, seal and deliver deeds about their ordinary relationship. They don't put them into writing. They don't even expressly say the one to the other, "I agree to pay you so much a week for the child", and the other to the one, "I accept." But they both know that an affiliation order can be obtained if the father does not support the child. And, in this case, we know from the jocular conversation in bed that both parties were well aware of the legal position. That being so, all that happens is all you'd expect to happen, namely that the father pays the mother so much a week.'

'He didn't divide the amounts, I gather,' said the judge. 'He didn't say "here is ten pounds for yourself and five pounds for Hugh". He just handed over a lump sum.'

'That is true,' said Miss Frayling. 'But obviously a reasonable amount of that sum was intended for the support of the infant. Mrs West accepted it. You don't require any particular form to make most kinds of agreement in this country. As my learned friend says, a person can go into a flat without any agreement, written or by word of mouth, and start paying rent. The amount of rent need not even have been agreed beforehand. If the

188

landlord accepts it week by week a tenancy is created. A dumb man could point out to a gardener his lawn and lawn mower. The gardener mows the lawn each Monday and is paid an amount each time. That would make an agreement by the one to employ the other to mow the lawn. Here the mother has a legal right to have the child maintained by the father, but there was, of course, a limit to the amount which the court could allow. Many fathers would prefer to pay a larger sum than was legally necessary in order to avoid court proceedings. In such a case, if the parties are on bad terms they will have a written agreement. But, if they are still lovers, no express agreement is necessary. In my submission, Mr West has proved his case on this point and it would be a denial of justice if an innocent man who has suffered so much through no fault of his own should be deprived of the right at least to be heard on whether this order should be set aside.

'Should your Honour dismiss this application at this stage the position will be this. A man who was wrongly sent to prison will have been deprived of the right to be heard on the question whether his son should be taken away from him, partly through a false statement made by Mrs West and partly, I must submit, through the casual way in which the adoption society, and the guardian, and, with the greatest respect and without intending to be impertinent, the Court itself dealt with the situation of the putative father. Having been deprived of that right when the adoption proceedings originally took place, he is now to be turned away from the judgment seat without being allowed to say a word. If that is the law, your Honour, it certainly is not justice. And I feel sure that, in this court, your Honour would always wish justice to prevail if that is possible.'

'That is so, I am sure, in every court in this country, Miss Frayling,' said the judge. 'I don't think this preliminary point is at all an easy one. Although I originally said I should decide it first, I shall exercise a privilege which is said to belong to the learned advocates in this case, and change my mind. I shall hear the whole case before giving a decision on any part of it.'

So Randolph was recalled into the witness box. First of all he told how he had met Margaret, and said that it was only after the child's birth that he had fallen in love with her. It was only two months after the child's birth that he went to live with Margaret and she became known as Mrs West. He described their year of happiness. He then dealt with his arrest, conviction, and pardon.

'Mr West,' said Miss Frayling, 'we all know that you were in fact innocent but had you any means of proving where you were at the time of your trial?'

'My word.'

'But, apart from your word, was there any piece of evidence which you could call to show you were not guilty?'

'I don't quite follow. I was not guilty and said so.'

'Quite, but there was evidence against you apart from that which was planted on you.'

'There was a horrible series of coincidences.'

'Exactly,' said Miss Frayling. 'We all know them to be coincidences now, but no one at the time could be sure of that, except you, could they?'

'No.'

'And that included Mrs West, didn't it? She only had your word that you were innocent?'

'That is so.'

'You had no alibi, for example?'

'No.'

'So that, when the false evidence about the strands of material was given, do you think it was easy or difficult for Mrs West to believe in your innocence?'

'It must have been very difficult for her.'

Randolph spoke in moving terms and with some emotion of his love for Hugh, and of his desperate wish to have him back. No one in the room could have failed to have been moved by his obvious sincerity.

Mrs Boulder then began to cross-examine him.

'Mr West,' she began, 'we all know that in certain respects you are a very wronged man. Please don't think that I haven't that well in mind when I ask you some very unpleasant questions.'

'Thank you,' said Randolph.

'You have complained at not being served with these proceedings, but initially that's your fault, isn't it?'

'For giving a child to Miss Parton, I agree. I've admitted that already.'

'I'm not referring to that,' said Mrs Boulder, 'but to your conduct after you knew she was going to have a child.'

'I paid all the expenses.'

'You paid all the expenses,' repeated Mrs Boulder. 'Yes, you paid all the expenses. You were a grown man, you had amused yourself at a girl's expense and got her in the family way; did you think your responsibility consisted solely in paying the expenses?'

'What else could I have done?'

'Did you consider at the time what else you could have done?'

'I don't know that I did.'

'Well, perhaps you'd consider it now,' said Mrs Boulder. 'Did you ask the girl whether she'd like you to come and live with her?'

'No.'

'Later you did live with her?'

'Yes.'

'And she changed her name to West?'

'Yes.'

'You now wish to marry her after you are free?'

'Definitely.'

'Now, if you'd gone to live with her before the child was born, and she'd changed her name before its birth, it could have had both your names on the birth certificate.'

'That is so.'

'If you'd done that, the child could never have been put out for adoption without your knowing it, could it?'

'I suppose not.'

'Then whose fault was it initially that no one asked you whether you agreed to the adoption?'

'Isn't that for me to say?' interposed the judge. 'It doesn't matter what the view of the witness is, does it? What we want from the witness are the facts.'

'If your Honour pleases,' said Mrs Boulder. 'Well now, Mr West, you never even considered whether it would be for the benefit of the child if you went to live with the mother?'

'I didn't intend to marry her at the time.'

'That's frank at any rate,' said Mrs Boulder, 'but it doesn't show much consideration for your child, does it?'

'If you put it that way.'

'How would you put it?' asked Mrs Boulder.

'It wouldn't have done anyone any good for me to go and live with Margaret unless we loved each other.'

'It might have done the child some good. After all, you had been ready enough to sleep with the girl for your own purposes, you wouldn't have bound yourself to anything by going to live with her. You could always have left later and the child would have had the advantage of having two names on the birth certificate.'

'She could have done that anyway.'

'Really, Mr West,' said Mrs Boulder, 'are you seriously suggesting that a girl should change her name to that of a man she'd met once at a dance?'

'It would be quite a good idea,' said the judge, 'from the point of view of the child. If, later on, the two people did marry that would be fine. If they did not, the birth certificate would look no worse than one with a blank in the column for the father's name. It would show Margaret West as the mother and Randolph West as the father. The fact that the addresses were different might only suggest that the parties were living apart at the time of the birth. The child would appear legitimate. As it is, all that appears on the certificate is Margaret Parton "mother" and no father.'

'Did you suggest to Miss Parton that she should change her name before you went to live with her?'

'No.'

'Then you can't very well blame her for not thinking of it.'

'Of course I don't blame her.'

'But you never even tried to think if there was anything else you could do for the boy, besides paying for him to be brought into the world and to stay in it.'

'If I'd realised everything that was going to happen I might have acted differently.'

'I dare say, but, as it was, you considered your responsibility was discharged by paying money, like a man with a discarded mistress?'

'I don't like that way of putting it.'

'I dare say you don't,' said Mrs Boulder, 'but it's an apt comparison, isn't it? All you were going to do was pay.'

'I think you've made that point sufficiently, Mrs Boulder,' said the judge, intervening. 'But, as we're on the subject, I'm not at all sure that even in this day and age a man should stand in danger of losing his rights at law because he doesn't go and live in sin with a woman. It is still immoral and contrary to religious teaching to do so. Yet at the end of this case, when I'm weighing the rights and wrongs of the matter, you are going to ask me to put in the scales against Mr West that he didn't go and live with Miss Parton sooner than he did. Does adultery improve with its continuance?'

'In cases where marriage is impossible, it may well be that it does, your Honour,' said Mrs Boulder.

'Why not wait till marriage is possible? Why oughtn't Mr West to have waited until he could get a divorce, before going to live with Miss Parton?'

'If that had been his reason,' said Mrs Boulder, 'if he had said that he was ashamed of his one act of adultery and did not propose to repeat it, one could have respected such an attitude. But that was not at all the case with Mr West. As soon as he found that he loved Miss Parton or, as I might say more unkindly, wanted to sleep with her again, and she was available for the purpose, he went to live with her. No moral scruples there, your Honour.'

'Quite right, Mrs Boulder,' said the judge, 'but I'll still want a lot of convincing that the fact that a man did not go and live in adultery is to be held against him in a court of law.'

Mrs Boulder concluded her cross-examination. Miss Frayling did not re-examine, and Margaret was then called. In answer to Miss Frayling, she gave the history of her association with Randolph, of the birth of the child, and of her putting him out for adoption. She ended by saying that she wanted the child back.

Mrs Boulder's first question was: 'Is it you or Mr West who wants the child back more?'

'We both want him.'

'Equally?'

A slight hesitation, then, 'Yes,' said Margaret.

'Quite sure?'

'As far as I can tell.'

'You gave your consent to the adoption freely?'

'I did. I was in a terrible state at the time.'

'But no one tried in any way to persuade you?'

'No.'

'It was you all along who wanted the child to be adopted?'

'Yes. It was a dreadful position to be in. I did what I thought was right.'

'You thought it right to lie to the authorities?'

'I had to. Mr West would never have agreed.'

'So you deceived everyone?'

'Yes. Which is the worse – to lie or to give a baby no fair chance in life? That was my problem. There *are* worse things than telling lies, your Honour, and in my view to have kept Hugh in the circumstances would have been one of them. Sometimes it must be right to lie and I still think I was right in this case to do so.'

'But, as a result of your deception, my clients have brought this child up as their own for two years, whereas, if you'd told the truth, that wouldn't have happened.'

'I know. I'm more sorry than I can say. But I couldn't tell what was going to happen, could I? Of course I wouldn't have let Hugh go if I had had any idea that Randolph would be pardoned.'

'Your regrets wouldn't be much consolation to Mr and Mrs Woodthorpe if they lost the child now, would they?'

'I suppose not.'

'Have you considered at all the effect upon the child if you have him back?'

'Of course I have.'

'And what effect d'you think it will have?'

'He may be unhappy for a time, but we *are* his real parents and he *was* with us for a year, and I think he will soon get used to us again, and be happy.'

'Supposing an eminent psychiatrist were to say that it might be dangerous for the child to return to you, would that alter your view?'

'In what way dangerous?'

'Supposing he just said dangerous?'

'Then I'd ask him what he meant by it.'

Mrs Boulder smiled.

'You're quite right,' she said. 'Supposing he said that the boy might develop serious neuroses when he grew older?'

'I'm told that this may happen to any child, however brought up.'

'But if you were told by a doctor you trusted that to take this child back might give it a greater chance of suffering from a neurosis than if he stayed where he was, would that change your mind about asking for the child back?'

'If I believed that the child would come to harm by returning to us, I should not ask for this to be done. But it would take more than one doctor to make me believe this, even if he were a doctor whom I trusted. I trust my dentist, but he has sometimes hurt me unnecessarily. At least I believe it was unnecessary. If every doctor said the same, that would be different. But we are calling a doctor who says that Hugh is unlikely to come to any harm if he comes back to us.'

'Now, of course, you've talked this matter over with Mr West?'

'Naturally.'

'There seems no doubt at all that Mr West is desperately attached to the child?'

'That is absolutely true.'

'He would do anything legal to get the child back?'

'Certainly.'

'Have you ever talked over with him the possible danger to the child of having him back?'

'Yes, I have.'

'Who raised the question first, you or he?'

Margaret hesitated.

'I couldn't be sure. I think *I* did.'

'And what was his reaction?'

'That everything would be all right.'

'That was his immediate reaction when this question arose?'

'Yes.'

'Was it yours?'

'I agreed with him.'

'Immediately?'

'We discussed the matter, and I agreed with him.'

'Well then, if it was you who first raised the matter, you must have had some doubt about it?'

'It naturally occurred to me, and I thought it right to talk about it to Randolph.'

'Would it be right to say, then, that before this application was made, you wondered whether it would be good for the boy to have him back?'

'Yes.'

'And you then mentioned it to Mr West?'

'Yes.'

'Are you sure of this?'

'Yes.'

'Quite sure?'

'Yes.'

'Then why, when I asked you who first raised this question, did you say: "I can't be sure. I think *I* did." '

'I wasn't sure then, but I am now. I don't suppose you've ever been in a witness box, Mrs Boulder. It's not easy to be sure on the spur of the moment.'

'Very well, then,' said Mrs Boulder, 'will you tell me this? Mr West will be heartbroken if this application fails. Will you?'

'I shall be terribly upset.'

'But not as upset as Mr West?'

'I haven't had two years in prison dreaming of a child who wasn't there.'

'And whose fault were those dreams?'

'Mine,' said Margaret, 'but I think I was right at the time. What chance in life would the boy have with a father under a ten-year sentence for a crime of this kind?'

'I asked you if you would be as upset as Mr West would be, if this application failed. You didn't answer directly, but do I rightly assume from your answer that you would not be as upset as he would be?'

'That is true,' said Margaret, 'but you must understand that I underwent my ordeal two years ago, when I gave Hugh away. I was heartbroken then. And it was a terrible ordeal to have to pretend he was still with me. But one does somehow get used to things. I shall be most unhappy if Hugh does not come back to us. I loved him dearly, and still do. I shall be even more unhappy because of the pain to Randolph after all he has suffered already.'

'Do you think you will suffer more than Mr and Mrs Woodthorpe if the boy they dote on is suddenly snatched from them?'

'I know of no way of measuring suffering,' said Margaret. 'Two people are going to be made desperately unhappy by the order in this case.'

'It could be three, couldn't it?' said Mrs Boulder. 'You've forgotten Hugh.'

And, like a good dramatist, Mrs Boulder made that her exit line. Miss Frayling did not re-examine, and called her next witness.

This was Dr Bream, a psychiatrist. In order to give the doctors an opportunity of meeting Hugh without upsetting him or making him self-conscious, it had been arranged that there should be a tea party at the Woodthorpes, which they attended. They were thus able to see him in his normal surroundings and casually ask him anything which they thought might be of value.

Dr Bream took the oath and sat in the witness chair. First he gave a list of his qualifications. They were impressive.

'Dr Bream,' said Miss Frayling, 'before I ask you about the particular boy in this case, I should like to ask you some general questions.'

'By all means.'

'Generally speaking, is it better for a child to be in the same home until it is grown up?'

'That depends on the home, madam,' said the doctor.

'Dr Bream,' said the judge, 'you are used to giving evidence, I believe?'

'Indeed yes, your Honour.'

'Then no doubt you are used to listening to the question before you answer it?'

'Of course, your Honour.'

'Did you not hear Miss Frayling say "generally speaking" in her question?'

'I did, your Honour.'

'Then did you not realise from that expression that Miss Frayling was excluding cases where the father came home drunk every night or the mother took drugs? She was referring to the ordinary decent household in this country, households where psychiatrists are never required.'

Although Dr Bream had laid himself open to this attack, he was not taking the very last of the judge's remarks without a fight.

'Your Honour would be surprised at the number of households where our services are required. Unfortunately we are often not sent for, with lamentable results.'

'Indeed?' said the judge. 'Now would you be kind enough to answer Miss Frayling's question. Perhaps you'd repeat it, Miss Frayling?'

'No need, thank you,' said Dr Bream. 'I remember it perfectly. And the answer is "yes".'

'But I've forgotten the question,' said the judge. 'So "yes" means nothing to me.'

'Generally speaking,' said Dr Bream, slightly emphasising the words, 'generally speaking,' he repeated, 'it is better for a child to be brought up in one home.'

'It hardly requires your eminent services to tell us that,' said the judge.

'I was asked the question,' said Dr Bream, 'and I understand that it is contempt of court not to answer.'

'It is also contempt of court to try to be funny in the witness box, Dr Bream,' said the judge. 'Now let's get on, Miss Frayling.'

'Have you known many cases of children who for one reason or another have changed from one home to another at an early age, say the age of three or thereabouts?'

'Yes, I have,' said Dr Bream.

'What percentage of these children have, in your view, suffered in any way from the change?'

'I can't be dogmatic about it, but I should say about fifty per cent.'

'So it is an even chance,' asked the judge, 'that a child who changes its home at the age of three will suffer in consequence?'

'I didn't say so, your Honour.'

'Did you not say "about fifty per cent"?'

'Certainly.'

'That's an even chance.'

'It is, your Honour.'

'Then why do you say to me that you didn't say it was an even chance that a child who changes its home at the age of three will suffer in consequence?'

'Because I didn't say it, your Honour.'

'Really, doctor, perhaps I'm in need of your attention, but you have made two completely opposite statements.'

'No,' said Dr Bream, 'I have not.'

'Let me try again,' said the judge. 'Did you not say fifty per cent, and is that not an even chance?'

'Certainly, your Honour.'

'But now you say you didn't say it.'

'I did say that, your Honour.'

'Then you agree that fifty per cent of children who are moved from one home to another at the age of three suffer in consequence?'

'No, your Honour. I did not say it and I do not believe it to be true.'

'Miss Frayling, would you be good enough to elucidate?' said the judge.

'I think,' began Miss Frayling, 'that what the doctor means ...'

But Mrs Boulder interrupted.

'I should be obliged if the doctor will tell us himself what he means without being led by Miss Frayling.'

'Very well, Dr Bream,' said Miss Frayling, 'will you tell the learned judge what you meant?'

'It's quite simple,' said Dr Bream. 'I said that about fifty per cent of the children whose cases I've known about have suffered through a change of home at an early age.'

The judge pushed his papers away from him in a gesture of annoyance. In fact he pushed them so far that Miss Frayling had very delicately to push them back again, or they would have become confused with her own.

'That is exactly what *I* said,' said the judge. 'And we've wasted five minutes getting there.'

'But with respect, your Honour,' said Dr Bream, 'it is not what you said.'

'I may or may not be in need of your services, doctor, but I am quite capable of remembering what I said a few minutes ago.'

'I'm very sorry to be persistent,' said Dr Bream, 'but your Honour said that I had said that fifty per cent of children moved at an early age from one home to another suffer in consequence.'

'And you have just admitted that you said that.'

'I have not, your Honour. I have agreed that fifty per cent of the children *whose cases I have known about* have suffered from a change of home. Many of the children I see are not normal children anyway. About half of these children have suffered as I've said. But I wouldn't at all agree that anything like that percentage of normal children would suffer.'

'I see,' said the judge, and remained silent for some time.

'What is your opinion of the likelihood of a normal child being injuriously affected by a change of home at the age of three?' asked Miss Frayling.

'Given a similar kind of home with similar standards and fond parents or foster-parents, I would say that very few normal children would come to any harm. I have had a case or two where the only definite fact we could ascertain was a change of environment at an early age but we could only guess that that was the cause of the trouble. It might have been something quite else. For a normal child, given the good conditions which I've mentioned, the risk of injury is very small indeed, far less than the risk of being run over in the streets or injured by accident at home.'

'Of course, if a child is not normal, different considerations will apply?'

'Naturally.'

'Or if the home to which it is sent is in certain respects unsatisfactory?'

'Agreed.'

'Now, you have seen this child once. Did you see enough of it to be able to say whether it is normal or not?'

'Well, I was told by Mr and Mrs Woodthorpe's doctor that physically he was absolutely normal. On that basis and from what I observed myself I would say unquestionably that Hugh is a normal, happy child.'

'Have you talked to Mr and Mrs West, to see what sort of people they are?'

'I have. I have interviewed them for a total period of five and a half hours. On different occasions, of course.'

'And what sort of people did you find them?'

'They have a high standard mentally. They seem to me to be well-balanced, kind people, who would give an admirable home to any child. Mr West is undoubtedly very strung-up at these proceedings. It would be strange if he were not. I was, however, much impressed by his self-control. Many normal men who had undergone his hardships and continued strain would not have stood up to them anything like as well as he has.'

'In your opinion, Dr Bream,' asked Miss Frayling, 'if Hugh goes back to his natural parents, is there any likelihood that he will have a less happy or useful life than if he stays where he is?'

'In my opinion,' said Dr Bream, 'there is not.'

'Thank you, Dr Bream,' said Miss Frayling. 'That is all I wish to ask.'

'Dr Bream,' asked Mrs Boulder, 'are you always as confident of your opinions as you appear to be in this case?'

'Certainly not. Sometimes I am far from confident.'

'You have given evidence in a good many cases, have you not?'

'I have.'

'Have you given evidence in cases where you felt far from confident?'

'Quite possibly.'

'When giving evidence in such cases, have you nevertheless appeared to be confident?'

'Like counsel, d'you mean?' said Dr Bream, and, like Oscar Wilde when he joked in cross-examination, immediately regretted it. He realised what was coming and it came.

'Yes,' said Mrs Boulder, 'like counsel.'

Dr Bream hesitated. If he agreed that expert witnesses were very like counsel, he would be admitting that he was an advocate rather than a witness. The certainty with which he had given his evidence would be discounted accordingly. Counsel are entitled to appear to have a firm belief in the righteousness of their client's cause, provided they make no false statement in the process. If he said expert witnesses were not at all like counsel, he would be asked why he raised the matter. And, confound it, he *had* raised the matter. After a little more thought he decided that there was only one way out. Otherwise he could see Mrs Boulder neatly folding him up and tying the string around him as though he were a brown paper parcel.

'I'm sorry, Mrs Boulder,' he said, 'I was joking.'

Mrs Boulder looked at him, paused for a moment and then said rather than asked: 'You were joking.'

'I'm afraid so.'

'I see,' said Mrs Boulder. 'This is a case where both parties are suffering a tremendous strain and where one side or the other is going to suffer great distress, and you thought it right in answer to one of my very first questions to make a joke.'

'I shouldn't have done so.'

'Perhaps you would tell me whether there were any other jokes in your evidence?'

'No, there were not. I repeat, I'm sorry about that one.'

Mrs Boulder, like the good bulldog she was, considered whether to have another bite at this particularly juicy piece of Dr Bream, or whether to try somewhere else. She decided not to spoil her first mouthful.

'Then perhaps we may return to the question, Dr Bream. In some cases where you have given evidence, but have been far from confident, have you appeared to be confident in giving your evidence?'

'I have tried to tell the truth.'

'Successfully, Dr Bream?' queried Mrs Boulder.

'I hope so.'

'No doubt, Dr Bream, but would you now mind answering my question directly?'

'I thought I had.'

Dr Bream was not enjoying himself. This bulldog showed every sign of not just nipping him round the ankle joints but of making a pretty good meal of him.

'I asked you if you had appeared confident in certain cases.'

'How can I tell how I appear to other people?' asked Dr Bream.

Mrs Boulder made a gesture of pushing away her papers from her, much as the judge had done. One of the disadvantages for advocates at hearings in a judge's private room is that the advocate remains seated while questioning the witness, and cannot therefore drop his papers on the desk as a gesture of impatience. But Mrs Boulder's substitute was quite effective.

'I rather prefer your jokes to your hedging, Dr Bream,' she said.

'I don't think you should talk to the witness like that, Mrs Boulder,' said the judge. 'Your right and duty is to ask questions, not to be offensive.'

'I'm sorry, your Honour,' said Mrs Boulder.

The witness was grateful for the respite. He was not used to being mauled in the very first round.

'Dr Bream,' said Mrs Boulder, 'I apologise for being offensive, but do you not agree that every professional advocate, witness or speaker, must know perfectly well whether he is giving an appearance of confidence when he speaks?'

'I suppose that is right.'

'Then why did you say to me "how can I tell how I appear to other people"?'

'Well, I can't be sure what impression I make on an audience.'

'Of course not, but you can be sure whether you've done yourself justice, made a good show, put your point across well, or however you like to phrase it?'

'Yes, I suppose so.'

'Then, when I asked you whether you appeared confident in certain cases when you gave evidence, why did you answer "How can I tell how I appear to other people?" '

'Well, it wasn't a very good answer.'

'Was it a joke or a hedge? I don't mean that question offensively. I want to know the answer.'

'It was certainly not a joke.'

'Then was it a hedge?'

'I hope I never hedge.'

'Then it couldn't have been a hedge?'

'No.'

'Then what was it? An honest answer?'

'An honest but stupid answer.'

Dr Bream was beginning to take off his clothes and hand them to the dog, in the hope that it would leave his flesh alone.

'Have any of your other answers been stupid?'

'That is not for me to say.'

'But it is, doctor,' persisted Mrs Boulder, flinging his discarded pants contemptuously aside. 'You yourself have described one of your answers as stupid. I want to know if you'd describe any of your other answers as stupid. Would you?'

'No.'

'None?'

'No.'

'What about the joke?' asked Mrs Boulder, putting her paw on the old wound just to keep it smarting.

'Yes, that was stupid. I'd forgotten.'

'You'd forgotten about the joke, Dr Bream?' asked Mrs Boulder incredulously.

'Well, not forgotten,' said Dr Bream. 'I hadn't got it in mind.'

'Well, bearing it in mind, Dr Bream, you have made two stupid answers in your evidence?'

'Yes.'

'D'you usually make two stupid answers when you are giving evidence, Dr Bream?'

'I don't think so.'

'But you have today?'

'Yes.'

'Would it be unfair to say, then, that you are being more than usually stupid in giving your evidence today?'

'Isn't that just being offensive, Mrs Boulder?' said the judge.

'Perhaps, your Honour,' said Mrs Boulder, 'but I do want to know if the doctor's having an off-day. If he is, his evidence can't count for very much, in my submission.'

The doctor decided to launch a counter-attack.

'I've never been cross-examined so offensively,' he said.

'I see,' said Mrs Boulder. 'So your stupid answers were due to offensive questions, were they?'

'They were asked offensively,' said Dr Bream.

'Let us see,' said Mrs Boulder, of whom Mr Luttrell had rightly said that, when she got her teeth into anything, she wouldn't let go. 'The first stupid answer you gave was in answer to my question "When giving evidence in such cases have you nevertheless appeared to be confident?" What was offensive about the question?'

Dr Bream began to regret his impetuosity. He handed a sock to his opponent.

'No, that question was not offensive.'

Mrs Boulder did not even sniff the sock.

'Was my manner in asking it offensive?'

'I can't say that it was.'

'Then your first stupid answer was not due to the offensiveness of my question?'

208

'Apparently not.'

'But you said it was.'

'That was a mistake.'

'Would it be fair to describe it as a stupid mistake?'

'No doubt you think so, Mrs Boulder.'

The dog opened its mouth wide preparatory to tasting a large piece of Dr Bream.

'It doesn't matter what I think,' said Mrs Boulder, 'but do you not, Dr Bream,' she asked with quiet emphasis, 'deeply regret having made that answer?'

There was little fight left in the doctor.

'Yes, I'm sorry I said it.'

'And are you not sorry because it was a stupid thing to say?'

'I suppose so.'

'So we now have three stupid answers. I take it that is most unusual, Dr Bream?'

'Yes.'

'Can you account for them? Perhaps you're not feeling quite yourself?'

'I have been working rather hard.'

'No doubt much too hard, doctor. I sympathise. Perhaps you'd prefer the learned judge not to take too much notice of your evidence, if you feel that on this occasion you haven't done yourself justice?'

'Not in answer to *your* questions.'

'So you'd like the learned judge to pay regard to your examination-in-chief but not your cross-examination?'

'Does it matter what the doctor wants? Have you much more to ask the witness?' said the judge. He felt like stopping the fight. The doctor was taking too much punishment.

'I have some more questions, your Honour,' said Mrs Boulder, 'and one of them is one of my early ones which still remains unanswered. In cases where you were not confident, doctor, have you not given evidence as though you were?'

'In every case I have given my honest opinion.'

'Confidently, or not?'

'As confidently as the nature of the case allowed,' said Dr Bream.

Why didn't I think of that answer before? he asked himself.

'That means that, when you did not feel confident about a matter, you made it plain in your evidence that you were not confident about it?'

'Precisely.'

'Now, this is not intended as an offensive question, doctor, but you were paid to give such evidence?'

'Yes.'

'Quite well paid?'

'My normal fees.'

'Which are not inconsiderable?'

'Must I answer such questions, your Honour?' the doctor appealed to the judge.

'I really don't see why you should,' said the judge.

'Very well,' said Mrs Boulder. 'Can you think of any reason in the world why a party to proceedings should pay you your usual fees to get you to give evidence that you were not at all confident in your opinion? That wouldn't be worth much, would it?'

'I didn't get up and say I wasn't confident in what I was saying.'

'But your manner and expressions or both showed that you weren't confident. That is what you've just said. "As confidently as the nature of the case allowed." And you agreed that you made it plain in your evidence that you were not confident in the matter. How did you make it plain except by your manner or what you said?'

Dr Bream no longer congratulated himself on this answer. He hadn't thought of it before because it was a rotten answer.

'I can't recall every case I've given evidence in,' he said lamely.

The dog sniffed and looked at the torn clothing and the mauled, naked body of the doctor. There was no need to bite any more for the moment. Mrs Boulder decided that a little astringent lotion applied to the wounds might do no harm.

'Dr Bream, I expect you know Dr Crestway, whom I shall be calling as a witness?'

Unfortunately Mrs Boulder's first choice, Dr Baldry, had been taken ill, while Dr Mallet was at a conference in America. So they had to risk Crestway. Having regard to the treatment Dr Bream had received, Dr Crestway looked a good bet, she thought, and then shivered. Bet, she had said. Mustn't mention anything like that to Dr Crestway.

'Yes, I know Dr Crestway,' said Dr Bream.

'He disagrees entirely about the effect of moving children of three from one home to another.'

'We often disagree,' said Dr Bream.

'But he is an eminent psychiatrist?'

'Certainly.'

'You have often heard him give evidence?'

'Yes, frequently.'

'And sometimes you have given evidence on opposite sides, as you are today? Was Dr Crestway always wrong when he disagreed with you?'

'I thought so, naturally.'

'Why "naturally"? We're all fallible. He might have convinced you that you were wrong. I take it that you are

211

open to argument? Of course you might convince him that he was wrong or *vice versa*?'

'Yes.'

'So you were open to being convinced by him that you were wrong?'

'Certainly.'

'Then why did you say, when I asked you if Dr Crestway was always wrong when he disagreed with you, that you "thought so *naturally*"?'

'Because I thought he was wrong.'

'Why did you use the word *naturally*?'

'I'm not sure.'

'It slipped out, didn't it? It meant that he was an advocate on one side and you were the advocate on the other and so *naturally* you didn't agree.'

'If you say so.'

'But d'you agree?'

'I suppose so.'

'Well, which did you mean, doctor? Do you mean that, when you give evidence in a case, you give your honest opinion and are prepared to admit that it is wrong if other evidence convinces you of that, or do you mean that, when you give evidence, you are going to back up the side you are fighting for and are *naturally* not going to alter your evidence?'

'I shouldn't have used the word "naturally".'

'Perhaps not, Dr Bream, but you did. Was that another stupid answer?'

Dr Bream did not answer, but the dog was satisfied and subsided, licking its lips.

'Any re-examination, Miss Frayling?' asked the judge.

'Dr Bream,' said Miss Frayling, 'my learned friend in asking you questions has, as far as I can recollect, asked you not a single question about this boy. Having heard her questions, are you still of the same opinion of the effect on the boy of being given back to his real parents?'

'I am,' said Dr Bream, and thankfully withdrew.

'That is the case for Mr West,' said Miss Frayling.

First Mary and then Bill gave evidence. They told how and why they came to adopt Hugh, of their great fondness for him, of his progress as a child and of the desperate unhappiness Mary in particular would suffer if they lost him. Randolph had told Miss Frayling casually of the conversation which he had had with Bill at Lord's, when Bill had almost admitted that he would not so mind giving up the child if it were not for Mary. This was a partial admission which at one stage could have been made use of by Miss Frayling with effect. Bill had been rather inclined to say in evidence that he wanted to keep the child as much as Mary. Just as Mrs Boulder had suggested to Margaret that she was not as anxious for the return of the child as Randolph, so Miss Frayling suggested to Bill that he was not as anxious to keep the child as Mary was.

Bill so desperately wanted to keep Mary happy that he stretched a point with his conscience and said that they were equally devoted to the boy.

'Mr Woodthorpe,' began Miss Frayling, 'did you not happen to meet my client at Lord's?'

'I did.'

At that moment Randolph got up from his seat and spoke to Miss Frayling. Although he had let slip to his advisers the conversation he had had with Bill, he was not prepared to allow a private chat at Lord's to be used against his opponent. He told this to Miss Frayling, who reluctantly dropped the subject.

Eventually both Mary and Bill completed their evidence and Dr Crestway was called. In answer to Mrs Boulder he said among other things: 'We are born, your Honour, with certain physical characteristics which can be developed or neglected but which can never be radically altered. Great sportsmen are born, not made. It is quite true that many people have physical characteristics which, if carefully and painstakingly developed, will result in their being, for example, better at a particular game than many of their fellows. But they will never be champions unless they start with the necessary physical equipment. The same applies to the brain. Unless a baby is born with the necessary mental equipment it will never reach the highest ranks with its brain. Fellows of All Souls are born, not made. Of course, you can get borderline cases with brain or body. In such cases extra development may compensate for the initial slight inferiority. But to be a top-class athlete or a Fellow of All Souls you must start with a certain minimum of physical or mental equipment, as the case may be. Without that minimum no training, no teaching will produce the desired result. So my first premise is that you cannot change substantially the brain or the body. You can only improve the material already there. This applies equally to human beings and animals.'

'I can understand that,' said the judge, 'and it sounds logical, but I don't at the moment see how it is going to help me in this case.'

'Your Honour will,' said Dr Crestway. 'I have said that you cannot change the brain or the body. But each human being consists of more than brain and body. I am not speaking from a religious point of view when I say that every baby born into the world has a soul. You may call it personality or psyche, if you wish, but it is just as much a part of the person as his brain or body. But there is a very great difference between the personality, as I prefer to call it, on the one hand, and the body and brain on the other.

214

The latter cannot be changed, the former can be. In the first years of a child's life – the Jesuits say up till seven – I would not be so dogmatic about the exact age, which might be only five or six or even less in some cases, and as late as eight in a few others – in those first years the personality is developed and may be changed this way or that. All sorts of things may happen to it which can have the most appalling consequences both to the child and to the people with whom it comes in contact in later life. Delicate as is the brain and the nervous system, the personality is an even more delicate part of our equipment. Medical science is not yet sufficiently advanced to show how and why the personality can be changed or affected but it is as true to say that it *can* be changed as it is to say that the brain can be injured by a knock on the head.'

The witness paused.

'Go on, please,' said the judge.

'Well, now,' went on Dr Crestway, 'given an ordinary normal baby, brought up in an ordinary normal way, the brain and body will come to no harm. But the delicate mechanism of the personality is such that, without anyone appreciating the fact, much harm can be done to a child's personality with lasting effects. Those effects may range from the merely inconvenient to the disastrous. Unfortunately we are not able to produce a book of rules which will tell parents how to ensure that their child's personality is not adversely affected by its upbringing. But there is no doubt that one apparently trifling experience can affect a child for life. One word spoken, one sight seen, and I am not referring to dramatic matters at all, but to such everyday occurrences as an angry word spoken by a man to his wife – complete strangers to the child – or a mild slap given to another child who had been naughty.

Everything a child sees or hears or otherwise experiences goes to the formation or alteration of its personality. I hope I am still being lucid, your Honour.'

'I am enjoying your lecture, doctor,' said the judge.

'Now there are many unfortunate people today who, as far as one can tell, are sound in brain and body but who suffer from neuroses of various kinds. These neuroses are sometimes comparatively innocuous but sometimes very grave indeed. Many of them are, in my opinion, a result of some experience of the adult during his formative years as a child. I have had apparently normal people in my care who, if they were in a house, could not go out of it. Or, if they were outside, could not go in. Such unfortunate people are often highly intelligent and will tell me that their, fear of going out of the house, or into it, as the case might be, is quite irrational. They know that no harm will come to them, and yet they have this desperate fear which makes them break out into a sweat and have a feeling of grave panic at the mere idea of stepping outside the front door. And this on a beautiful, peaceful day, when they know that no harm can come to them. These patients of mine come from every class of society, from those qualified to be Fellows of All Souls and from those who failed (and rightly) to pass their eleven-plus. The exact cause of these neuroses, which precipitate utter misery in the patients, in spite of the fact that they know there is no physical reason for them, we do not know. But we do know that their origin is something to do with the patients' personality. It must be. We can see that mind and body are sound. There is only one other part of a human being which can be sick. And we know this too, that sometimes the cause of this sickness is to be found in an early experience or early experiences of the patient as a child.

216

'Now, I have said that we can produce no books of rules to give to parents to enable them to bring up their children without injury to their personality. But we do know this. It is obvious, is it not, that violent action in a child's life should be avoided, if possible? I am not, of course, referring to physical violence, but to things like violent change. Such as, for example, a change of home. In some cases a change of home cannot be avoided. Both parents might be killed in an accident or the like. Indeed, I had a patient not long ago whose parents were killed in an air crash when she was four. She was brought up by a most kindly aunt and uncle and appears to have had as happy a childhood as was possible in the circumstances. But I have no doubt that the illness for which I was treating her was due to the appalling wrench suffered by the child's personality by her change of home. I am quite satisfied in my own mind that, unless it is unavoidable, the home of a child of tender years should never be changed.'

'What d'you say about this particular child?' asked Mrs Boulder, who was very happy to have let the doctor have his head, so long as the judge did not appear restive.

'I have seen the child, the parents and the adopters. If I may say so, they all appear admirably normal. I cannot, of course, say what harm may have already been done to the child by the wrench to its personality when its home was changed at the age of one. Let us hope he will be lucky. But in my view to give his personality another wrench by another change at the age of three would be a very wrong thing to do, very wrong indeed. If it were necessary it would, of course, have to be done, but I have no hesitation in saying that it would be most undesirable and may have deplorable results on the child in later years. I should make it plain that what I am saying reflects in no way on

217

the home which the real parents wish to provide. As far as loving care and good sense are concerned I am sure that it would be an admirable home – for any child but this. No home would be admirable for this boy except the one he at present enjoys.'

'Thank you, doctor,' said Mrs Boulder, and Miss Frayling began to cross-examine.

'You disagree with Dr Bream, I gather?'

'I do.'

'But do you think the child may be quite all right when he grows up, if he's left where he is?'

'I certainly hope so.'

'There is a reasonable chance of it?'

'Yes, there is a reasonable chance.'

'In spite of the first change?'

'I've already said so.'

'Then you can't be sure, doctor, that harm would come from a further change?'

'I cannot, of course, guarantee it, but a change at the age of three is more violent than a change at the earlier age. And for a child to be played about with like a shuttlecock appears to me to be highly undesirable. There are enough risks in life without imposing that on him.'

'But you must have known adults who, through some such accident as you mentioned, became orphans at an early age and who suffer from no neuroses?'

'That is so, but why take the risk?'

'Doctor,' said Miss Frayling, 'I'd be grateful if you'd just answer my questions instead of questioning me. You have known quite normal people who were orphaned at an early age?'

'Yes, but none who were orphaned twice. None whose parents died when they were one and whose foster parents died when they were three.'

218

'Presumably there are such people in the world.'

'I should imagine so.'

'But none of them patients of yours?'

'No.'

'So, for all you know, none of these twice-orphaned children have come to any harm – in the way of neuroses, I mean.'

'As I don't know of any such case I cannot say what their history has been.'

'Of course not. I imagine that you talk about cases to your colleagues; not by way of chitchat, I mean, but seriously for the benefit of everyone generally?'

'Of course.'

'In your time you must have had a good many colleagues?'

'Certainly.'

'Has any one of your colleagues ever mentioned to you a case of a twice-orphaned child who subsequently became a victim of a neurosis?'

'I shouldn't be surprised.'

'Can you recall a single instance?'

'I can't say that I can.'

'So that, as far as your evidence goes, you have not had experience yourself of a patient who was twice-orphaned as a child, and you know no one else who has?'

'I tell you, I can't recall.'

'Then it follows that you are not able to say that any such child has come to any harm in later years from a neurosis?'

'I think it very likely that such children have so suffered.'

'But that is surmise, doctor.'

'Surmise, but based on knowledge of human physiology in its widest sense.'

'What would you say the odds would be?'

'The odds?' repeated the doctor sharply – and Mrs Boulder felt slight apprehension.

'Yes,' said Miss Frayling, 'the odds on Hugh turning out all right if he goes back to his parents.'

The doctor hesitated, and began to look slightly like a horse being led quietly around the paddock, when he suddenly sees someone he doesn't like.

'Is it an even chance that he'll be all right, or two to one or ten to one against, or what?'

The doctor still said nothing, but Mrs Boulder sadly imagined that she could see the whites of his eyes and that he might buck at any moment.

'Put it in terms of percentages, if you prefer,' said Miss Frayling, and Mrs Boulder made a mental note to thank her opponent afterwards.

'I should *very much* prefer to put it in terms of percentages,' said the doctor so vehemently that Miss Frayling could not resist asking why.

'Because I don't like references to odds in any shape or form,' said the doctor quite fiercely.

The judge looked puzzled, and Miss Frayling decided that the matter was worth pursuing.

'What's the objection, doctor?' she asked, and Mrs Boulder feared that there was going to be no need to thank her opponent.

'Odds savour of the racecourse,' said the doctor.

'Quite so,' said Miss Frayling, innocently. 'So you don't like racing, doctor?'

'Must I answer that question?' asked the doctor.

'Well,' said the judge, 'I don't quite see the relevance but it doesn't seem to be a very harmful question. Why don't you like racing, doctor?'

'It's a conspiracy,' said the doctor.

'I beg your pardon,' said the judge. '*What* is a conspiracy?'

'The whole thing, your Honour,' said the doctor. 'It ought to be put down by the law.'

Poor Mrs Boulder could see the white flag up. He'll be off in a moment, she said to herself.

'It's the owners, trainers, jockeys and bookmakers,' the doctor went on, and tried to grip the judge's arm. But Judge Hazlewell just managed to avoid the embrace. 'They all conspire against you,' continued the doctor. 'An honest punter hasn't a chance. They get you on the racecourse, fill you up with drink, take your money, give you a bit back to ensnare you, and then rob you right, left and centre. It's a positive scandal and they're all in it together. Either the races are rigged, or the prices, or both. The whole thing's a fantastic swindle. I can prove it. The vets are in it too. Dope tests! Who takes them? Who sees the results? Every now and then they pretend to warn off a trainer or a jockey, but it's all part of the conspiracy to keep the public going. I know what I'm talking about, your Honour. I've been there. I've been fleeced like all the others. I tell you, the judges are in it too. No offence to your Honour. My horse won once. That, no doubt, was an accident. It had been arranged that another horse should. What happened? The judge gave the race to the other horse. They said in the Press that he mistook the number. Mistook the number! The Press are in it too. Look at the papers they sell. Midday editions, racing editions. Look at the tipsters. They're all laughing at you. I'm sorry, your Honour, but it's a scandal. I repeat, it ought to be put down by the law.'

'How much did you lose, doctor?' asked Miss Frayling.

'That's not the point,' said the doctor, who was now riderless and on his third circuit, the race being held up meanwhile. 'I can be as sporting as the next man. If you make a gamble, you know you may lose. But you want a fair chance. That's all I ask. A fair chance. But you just don't get one.'

Mrs Boulder decided to try to catch the doctor. She stood up to ask her question.

'Dr Crestway,' she said loudly, 'we're talking about Hugh West.'

But the doctor ran outside her.

'The name of the horse doesn't matter,' he said. 'It's the principle involved.'

Mrs Boulder sat down and realised that she must wait till he slowed down from exhaustion and could be quietly captured and taken back to the paddock.

The doctor galloped on for some distance, but eventually had to stop.

'Doctor,' said Miss Frayling, 'I assure you that my next question is not intended to be offensive, but did you have a happy childhood?'

'Very,' said the doctor, now meekly allowing himself to be led back to the stables.

'No change of home at an early age?'

'No.'

'Whom d'you consult for your own troubles?'

'As a matter of fact,' said Dr Crestway, 'it's Dr Bream.'

The judge knew that some psychiatrists suffered quite as badly as some of their patients, but he began to have a higher opinion of them than he had before, not so much for their learning as for their ability to preserve confidences absolutely. It must have been a great temptation to Dr Bream to tell Randolph's advisers that he himself was treating Dr Crestway for his little neurosis; but, until Dr Crestway himself mentioned it, it was obvious that no one knew.

CHAPTER TWENTY

The Decision

The evidence on both sides was now concluded and the
judge adjourned the hearing until the next day. As the
parties left the court, Jeremy took Margaret on one side.

'Can I see you alone?' he asked.

'Of course,' said Margaret. 'When?'

'Now, if I may.'

'I'll tell Randolph.'

She went and spoke to him and came back to Jeremy.
'Give me a cup of tea somewhere,' she said.

They walked in silence to a teashop, went in and sat
down.

'I'm afraid it's about my case, not yours,' said Jeremy,
'that I want to talk to you.'

'I guessed as much,' said Margaret. 'But how d'you think
ours is going?'

'Well, the old trick cyclists have pretty well cancelled
each other out. After their performances he can't take
much notice of either of them. You don't know how much
I want you to win. I believe I'd almost bribe the judge, if
that were possible. There's nothing I wouldn't do for you.'

She smiled at him.

'No one could have done more than you have. But I'm
worried about Randolph. D'you think we'll win?'

'I just don't know,' said Jeremy. 'Some judges give you an indication of what they're thinking, but Hazlewell's been just like an oyster. Not a clue. But, if my prayers can do it, you'll win all right.'

'Thank you,' she said. 'It's so little to say for what you've done.'

'I've done nothing. It's what you've done for me. D'you know, I've had the happiest time of my life since I met you. I know you don't love me – and, in a sort of way, I don't want you to. You've had enough complications in your life already. Randolph will get his divorce soon, and I want you to live happily ever after. I'm so grateful to you for showing me what real love, the best kind of love is. It does give me an ache sometimes, it's true, but I'm so happy to have known you, so happy to have been allowed to help you. I'm not a fool. I will fall in love with some girl some day, but I shall want something out of that love.'

'I hope you get it,' she said. 'You'll deserve it, and she'll be very lucky.'

'Oh, no, there'll be no question of deserts. Most love is like that. He wants it, she wants it, they have it. It's all very wonderful in its way, but it's not the best kind of love, the love I have for you. I just want you to know this; and to know that, if ever at any time, however long ahead it may be, I can help in any way you'll only have to ask. Telephone me, send me a cable, call on me, anything. If I'm alive and on my feet I'll be there.'

She took his hand.

'I'll always come to you,' she said, 'whatever happens, always to you. And now let's have a cup of tea, and talk about Dr Bream and Dr Crestway. Did you notice that Bream gave Crestway a lift?'

When the parties and their lawyers came before Judge Hazlewell the next day, he told them that he would like to see the child before giving a decision.

'I don't think it would be a good thing for him to be brought here,' he said. 'So, subject to anything counsel may say, I propose that I adopt the same course as the psychiatrists. As far as seeing the child is concerned, I mean. I suggest that counsel and I go to Mr and Mrs Woodthorpe's this afternoon, as though we were paying an ordinary call.'

Both parties agreed to the judge's suggestion, and at half past three Mrs Boulder, Miss Frayling and the judge arrived at the Woodthorpes' house. After they had been there a few minutes Hugh was brought in to meet them.

'I see you have a swimming pool in your garden,' the judge said to the boy.

'It's a paddle pool really,' said Hugh, 'but Daddy says we'll have a proper pool when I'm older.'

'D'you want to swim?' asked the judge.

'Fishes swim,' said Hugh.

'Would you like to be a fish?' asked the judge.

Hugh shook his head.

'Mummy had a swimming pool in her garden when she was a little boy,' he confided.

Half an hour later the judge and counsel left and went back to the court. The judge offered to sit late to avoid another adjournment. First Mrs Boulder addressed him and then Miss Frayling. They each made forcibly the points which good advocates would have been expected to make and at the end the judge gave judgment.

'This is a lamentable case,' he began, 'in which great distress has been caused to both parties. Most of it was in my view unnecessary. Having seen Mrs West in the witness box, I am quite satisfied that, had she been brought here in the first instance and questioned about the child's parentage, she would have told the truth. Indeed, had she been pressed about the matter by the guardian or the adoption society, I fully believe that the truth would probably have emerged. In which case, although Mr and Mrs West might have suffered some unhappiness or even distress, it would have been nothing to what both sides have now suffered. And one side will continue to suffer. Unfortunately, in my opinion, insufficient care was taken to be sure of the position of the putative father. Often a putative father has no rights at all and would not care if he had, but that does not mean to say that care should not be taken to find out, as far as reasonably can be done, whether the putative father in each case has or has not a right to be heard on the matter. It is always possible that a mother may lie about the putative father. Normally she has no reason to do so, but it is far, far better for those concerned to take a little extra time over satisfying themselves that there is no putative father in the case with a right to be heard than to do what has happened here. If there is only one chance in a hundred thousand, why should the unnecessary risk be taken?

'The mere use of a serial number is no protection whatever to the adopters from an application to set aside the order. It is normally a protection against blackmail, but even then the information may by chance be learned by a criminal, or conceivably a mistake may be made by the Court, as in this case. I mention blackmail not because Mr or Mrs West are the sort of people to do anything of that kind. Subject to certain qualifications, they are people of the utmost respectability. But who was to know that they were? And, indeed, Mr West was in jail at the time, presumed to be a criminal.

'There may be cases where an adoption order seems very desirable but where the mother out of spite might change her mind and withdraw her consent if pressed about the putative father. If it could be proved that she withdrew her consent out of spite the Court could still make the adoption order, but in some cases spite might be difficult to prove. In such cases, no doubt, it would be right to weigh up the risks involved. If the adopters preferred to risk the sudden appearance of a putative father rather than the possibility of the mother changing her mind, it might be proper not to press the mother with further questions. But in the normal case it is in my view quite wrong for the possibility of there being rights in a putative father to be dismissed as lightly as it has been here. Indeed, it would have been far better for the mother to have changed her mind at a very early stage in this case than for the present situation to have arisen.

'Now, as to the application itself, I have heard the whole of the evidence, although it is only if Mr West can prove he is liable under an agreement to contribute to the maintenance of the child that he has any right to have the order set aside. Having heard all the evidence, I am going to give my opinion upon the case as a whole. In other words, I am going to express my view as to whether this child ought to go back to its real parents. If I or the Court of Appeal set aside the order and the application for adoption were heard again, I should have to bear in mind that the mother has now withdrawn her consent, and, unless I were satisfied that she had done so unreasonably, I could not make an adoption order, even if I thought it in the interests of the child to do so. It is perhaps strange that the legislature has leaned more in favour of a parent's rights than of a child's interests. But I have to abide by the law, and, however much an adoption order may be in the

interests of a child, the order cannot be made in the
absence of the mother's consent, or, if the child is
legitimate, in the absence of the father's consent too,
unless such consents are unreasonably refused or in a very
few special cases, none of which arise here.

'Now, there is no doubt that life has been very hard on
Mr West. He has suffered through no fault of his own in a
way for which he cannot be properly compensated. And it
was during his absence in prison, when he was unable to
fight for himself, that this child, to whom he is and always
has been utterly devoted, was given away. It was given
away because the mother lied about the child's parentage.
That again was no fault of the father, but those lies,
whether excusable or not, have been the main cause of
this tragedy.

'One can appreciate Mrs West's despair at the time, and
I am certainly not condemning her for what she did. She
made a great sacrifice to do what she thought was right.
But, when one has to compare the situation of the
adoptive parents – who took the child in good faith and
lavished all their love and care upon it – I cannot avoid
paying attention to the fact that it was the mother's lies
which, however understandable, even perhaps justifiable,
were the cause of the trouble. As far as the adoptive
parents are concerned, no fault can be found in them of
any kind. As far as the putative father is concerned, the
only criticism which can validly be made is that he is a
putative father. That is to say, that he chose to have
relations with a woman out of wedlock. In such cases
suffering may be caused. In most cases it is not the father
who suffers, but in a rare case, such as this, where it is the
father who suffers most, how can he legitimately
complain? There is to my mind no question at all that,
although no one could fail to feel the deepest sympathy

with Mr West, his and Mrs West's merits are not as great as Mr and Mrs Woodthorpe's.

'It would be wholly wrong of me if I tried to compensate Mr West for his false imprisonment by giving him back the child. That is his grave misfortune, but, because he has been wronged, that is no reason for transferring the burden to wholly innocent people. So much for the merits of the parties. As to the child itself, I am bound to say that, having seen him in his present surroundings, it would have taken a great deal to persuade me that he should be taken away from them. Had it been necessary to do this, I should have done so most reluctantly and with a heavy heart. It may be that Dr Bream is right and that he would get over the change without any ill effects. It may be that Dr Crestway is right and that he might be injured in his personality in consequence. But neither the evidence of the one or the other convinced me that the view of either was the right one. And I prefer to decide this case on what I have seen and heard of the parties themselves and the child, and not upon the theoretical evidence of the eminent gentlemen to whose evidence I have had the good fortune to listen.

'Looking at the matter broadly, I am quite satisfied that the child ought to remain where it is. From the purely legal point of view also I think that Mr West's application should fail. He was in my view a putative father who was not liable under any agreement to support the child. Had he withdrawn his support, he could have had an affiliation order made against him, but he could not have been sued under any agreement. In other words, this father never had the right to be served with the proceedings, though, of course, had the Court been aware of his existence, he certainly would have been served with them. The result is that this application fails, and the adoption order will remain. But I am sure that it was far better for me to hear the whole case and not simply to dismiss it on the technical ground that Mr West was not liable under an agreement to support the child. Had I done so, he would always have felt that his case had never been fully heard.

'In coming to my conclusions I have, of course, borne in mind the fact that, if and when Mr West obtains a divorce from his present wife, he and Mrs West will marry, and that on their marriage the child will become legitimate. I accept that a divorce is likely in the near future and I feel sure that Mr and Mrs West will marry when a decree is granted. But legitimate children can be adopted as well as illegitimate, and, though in the normal way one would hesitate a long time before taking away their child from legitimate parents, this is by no means a normal case. I am glad to think that the child may soon be legitimised, but that fact should not in my opinion alter my judgment.

'There is one further matter which I think I should mention. Nothing could compensate Mr and Mrs Woodthorpe for the loss of this child. They cannot have children of their own and Hugh has become, as near as it is possible, a child of their own. No doubt they could adopt another child, but that would not make up for the loss of this one. The real parents, however, who, I hope, may soon be happily married, can have a further child or children and I hope that they will do so. Mr West has shown so far great courage and control in adversity and I desire to express my earnest wish that for his own sake and for the sake of Mrs West he will accept this further undeserved calamity in his life with as much philosophical restraint as is possible.'

Just after the parties had left the judge's room, he sent a message to both counsel that he would like to see them. So Mrs Boulder and Miss Frayling returned.

'Do please sit down,' he said.

He did not say anything further for a short time. Eventually he said: 'Some people think that I do not approve of women at the Bar. That is quite wrong. I am delighted to see them in court, particularly, if I may say so, when they do their work as brilliantly as both of you do.'

They thanked him by a smile.

'But I must confess,' he went on, 'that for the first time I am a little embarrassed. In other words, I could say to you much more easily what I want to say if you were men.'

'I hope you will say it just the same, judge,' said Mrs Boulder. 'If you could hear the horrible language we have to use in court sometimes – by way of repeating what someone else has said, I mean – it might make you less worried about it.'

'It wouldn't,' said the judge. 'I have occasionally heard a woman member of the Bar appearing in a nuisance case, and I must confess that I'm old-fashioned enough to dislike very much hearing one of your sex say things like: "Now, Mr Jones, did you then say: You why don't you take your — to some other — ?" It's old age, I suppose.'

'Well, if it's any consolation to you, judge, my husband and I, who are on the best possible terms, often use what you would consider the most dreadful language to each other in the friendliest possible way. A lot of husbands and wives do.'

'But – Miss Frayling ...' the judge began. Miss Frayling interrupted: 'I'm married too, judge,' she said. 'I use my maiden name for professional purposes. I am afraid I can entirely confirm what my learned colleague has said. My husband and I not only know the facts of life, but we sometimes talk about them in the crudest language to each other. Not, of course, when we can be overheard, though we've nearly slipped up about that occasionally.'

'Well, it's nice of you to try to put me at my ease,' said the judge. 'I'm very worried about this case. Not about my decision which, whatever Miss Frayling may think, I feel sure is right. But about your unfortunate client. I don't think he'll do anything desperate but, of course, he might. And that would be a great tragedy. But I do feel he needs immediate help. They ought to have another child as quickly as possible. And I mean as quickly as possible. Nine months from today, if that could be arranged. This may sound odd coming from me, because they're still living in adultery. But, before the child is born, they will be married, and, if West can be given this early interest of a child being on the way and then its birth, I think he will eventually be able to overcome the distress from which be is now suffering. Well, now, why do I ask you? I couldn't, of course, see one of you here without the other. But it's Miss Frayling who is really concerned. Do try to get hold of your clients and persuade them of this. I know I said it in court, but I couldn't go into details then and coming at the end of what for them was a terrible judgment they may hardly have heard it. Possibly you could speak to Mrs West by herself?

'It's the urgency which I have in mind. A man in West's position might go into a fit of depression which could last for a very long time. I don't want another patient for Dr Bream or his patient Dr Crestway. Please do what you can. The Woodthorpes must have suffered terribly, too, but they will be all right for the future except for the scars. But West can recover too, if only he'll move quickly. I feel sure that a man with his possessive sense will take to a new baby as he took to the first. And, once he has another

232

baby, he can be comforted about the first because it is in good hands, could not be in better. But that comfort can never arise until he has one of his own on which to lavish all his love and hopes.'

'I do so agree,' said Miss Fraying. 'I was even thinking of inviting the Wests and my solicitor out to dinner, filling them up with champagne, sending them home, and hoping for the best. But I hardly felt I could do it now. It would seem like a celebration.'

'I am so glad,' said the judge. 'I can see that I'm preaching to the converted. I apologise for even indirectly suggesting that you wouldn't have thought of it yourself. It is, of course, the obvious answer. If by any chance you have any news in a year's time, I'd be very grateful if you'd pass it on.'

'Of course, judge,' said Miss Frayling. 'I'll try to get my solicitor to find out and let me know. And I'll tell you at once.'

'Thank you very much,' said the judge, 'and thank you both for your help in this very unhappy case.'

Mrs Boulder and Miss Frayling left the judge. He sat in his chair for half an hour, apparently doing nothing. Suddenly, without a knock, the door opened and his clerk walked in.

'Oh – I'm so sorry,' said the clerk. 'I thought your Honour had left.'

'That's quite all right,' said the judge. 'I was just – just thinking.'

He could not very well say to his clerk that he was praying for a baby for Randolph and Margaret.

While Judge Hazlewell had been occupied in this way, Judge Bramcote was dealing with another adoption case. The applicants sat anxiously waiting for his decision.

'I gather we don't know who the putative father is,' he said to their solicitor.

'That is so, your Honour,' said the solicitor.

'Well, I don't suppose he minds or cares,' said Judge Bramcote. 'I shall make this order with much pleasure, and I hope your clients will be very happy.'

HENRY CECIL

ACCORDING TO THE EVIDENCE

Alec Morland is on trial for murder. He has tried to remedy the ineffectiveness of the law by taking matters into his own hands. Unfortunately for him, his alleged crime was not committed in immediate defence of others or of himself. In this fascinating murder trial you will not find out until the very end just how the law will interpret his actions. Will his defence be accepted or does a different fate await him?

THE ASKING PRICE

Ronald Holbrook is a fifty-seven-year-old bachelor who has lived in the same house for twenty years. Jane Doughty, the daughter of his next-door neighbours, is seventeen. She suddenly decides she is in love with Ronald and wants to marry him. Everyone is amused at first but then events take a disturbingly sinister turn and Ronald finds himself enmeshed in a potentially tragic situation.

'The secret of Mr Cecil's success lies in continuing to do superbly what everyone now knows he can do well.'
The Sunday Times

HENRY CECIL

BRIEF TALES FROM THE BENCH

What does it feel like to be a Judge? Read these stories and you can almost feel you are looking at proceedings from the lofty position of the Bench.

With a collection of eccentric and amusing characters, Henry Cecil brings to life the trials in a County Court and exposes the complex and often contradictory workings of the English legal system.

'Immensely readable. His stories rely above all on one quality – an extraordinary, an arresting, a really staggering ingenuity.'
New Statesman

BROTHERS IN LAW

Roger Thursby, aged twenty-four, is called to the bar. He is young, inexperienced and his love life is complicated. He blunders his way through a succession of comic adventures including his calamitous debut at the bar.

His career takes an upward turn when he is chosen to defend the caddish Alfred Green at the Old Bailey. In this first Roger Thursby novel Henry Cecil satirizes the legal profession with his usual wit and insight.

'Uproariously funny.' *The Times*

'Full of charm and humour. I think it is the best Henry Cecil yet.' P G Wodehouse

HENRY CECIL

HUNT THE SLIPPER

Harriet and Graham have been happily married for twenty years. One day Graham fails to return home and Harriet begins to realise she has been abandoned. This feeling is strengthened when she starts to receive monthly payments from an untraceable source. After five years on her own Harriet begins to see another man and divorces Graham on the grounds of his desertion. Then one evening Harriet returns home to find Graham sitting in a chair, casually reading a book. Her initial relief turns to anger and then to fear when she realises that if Graham's story is true, she may never trust his sanity again. This complex comedy thriller will grip your attention to the very last page.

SOBER AS A JUDGE

Roger Thursby, the hero of *Brothers in Law* and *Friends at Court*, continues his career as a High Court judge. He presides over a series of unusual cases, including a professional debtor and an action about a consignment of oranges which turned to juice before delivery. There is a delightful succession of eccentric witnesses as the reader views proceedings from the Bench.

'The author's gift for brilliant characterisation makes this a book that will delight lawyers and laymen as much as did its predecessors.' *The Daily Telegraph*

OTHER TITLES BY HENRY CECIL AVAILABLE DIRECT
FROM HOUSE OF STRATUS

Quantity		£	$(US)	$(CAN)	€
☐	ACCORDING TO THE EVIDENCE	6.99	11.50	15.99	11.50
☐	ALIBI FOR A JUDGE	6.99	11.50	15.99	11.50
☐	THE ASKING PRICE	6.99	11.50	15.99	11.50
☐	BRIEF TALES FROM THE BENCH	6.99	11.50	15.99	11.50
☐	BROTHERS IN LAW	6.99	11.50	15.99	11.50
☐	THE BUTTERCUP SPELL	6.99	11.50	15.99	11.50
☐	CROSS PURPOSES	6.99	11.50	15.99	11.50
☐	DAUGHTERS IN LAW	6.99	11.50	15.99	11.50
☐	FRIENDS AT COURT	6.99	11.50	15.99	11.50
☐	FULL CIRCLE	6.99	11.50	15.99	11.50
☐	HUNT THE SLIPPER	6.99	11.50	15.99	11.50
☐	INDEPENDENT WITNESS	6.99	11.50	15.99	11.50
☐	MUCH IN EVIDENCE	6.99	11.50	15.99	11.50

ALL HOUSE OF STRATUS BOOKS ARE AVAILABLE FROM GOOD BOOKSHOPS OR
DIRECT FROM THE PUBLISHER:

Internet: www.houseofstratus.com including author interviews, reviews, features.

Email: sales@houseofstratus.com please quote author, title and credit card details.

OTHER TITLES BY HENRY CECIL AVAILABLE DIRECT
FROM HOUSE OF STRATUS

Quantity		£	$(US)	$(CAN)	€
☐	NATURAL CAUSES	6.99	11.50	15.99	11.50
☐	NO BAIL FOR THE JUDGE	6.99	11.50	15.99	11.50
☐	NO FEAR OR FAVOUR	6.99	11.50	15.99	11.50
☐	THE PAINSWICK LINE	6.99	11.50	15.99	11.50
☐	PORTRAIT OF A JUDGE	6.99	11.50	15.99	11.50
☐	SETTLED OUT OF COURT	6.99	11.50	15.99	11.50
☐	SOBER AS A JUDGE	6.99	11.50	15.99	11.50
☐	TELL YOU WHAT I'LL DO	6.99	11.50	15.99	11.50
☐	TRUTH WITH HER BOOTS ON	6.99	11.50	15.99	11.50
☐	UNLAWFUL OCCASIONS	6.99	11.50	15.99	11.50
☐	THE WANTED MAN	6.99	11.50	15.99	11.50
☐	WAYS AND MEANS	6.99	11.50	15.99	11.50
☐	A WOMAN NAMED ANNE	6.99	11.50	15.99	11.50

ALL HOUSE OF STRATUS BOOKS ARE AVAILABLE FROM GOOD BOOKSHOPS OR
DIRECT FROM THE PUBLISHER:

Hotline: UK ONLY: 0800 169 1780, please quote author, title and credit card
details.
INTERNATIONAL: +44 (0) 20 7494 6400, please quote author, title,
and credit card details.

Send to: House of Stratus
24c Old Burlington Street
London
W1X 1RL
UK

<u>Please allow following carriage costs per ORDER</u>
<u>(For goods up to free carriage limits shown)</u>

	£(Sterling)	$(US)	$(CAN)	€(Euros)
UK	1.95	3.20	4.29	3.00
Europe	2.95	4.99	6.49	5.00
North America	2.95	4.99	6.49	5.00
Rest of World	2.95	5.99	7.75	6.00
Free carriage for goods value over:	50	75	100	75

PLEASE SEND CHEQUE, POSTAL ORDER (STERLING ONLY), EUROCHEQUE, OR
INTERNATIONAL MONEY ORDER (PLEASE CIRCLE METHOD OF PAYMENT YOU WISH TO USE)
MAKE PAYABLE TO: STRATUS HOLDINGS plc

Order total including postage:_____Please tick currency you wish to use and
add total amount of order:

☐ £ (Sterling)　☐ $ (US)　☐ $ (CAN)　☐ € (EUROS)

VISA, MASTERCARD, SWITCH, AMEX, SOLO, JCB:

☐☐☐☐☐☐☐☐☐☐☐☐☐☐☐☐☐☐☐☐☐☐☐

Issue number (Switch only):

☐☐☐

Start Date:　　　　　　Expiry Date:

☐☐/☐☐　　　　　☐☐/☐☐

Signature: _____

NAME: _____

ADDRESS: _____

_____

POSTCODE: _____

Please allow 28 days for delivery.

Prices subject to change without notice.
Please tick box if you do not wish to receive any additional information. ☐

House of Stratus publishes many other titles in this genre; please
check our website (**www.houseofstratus.com**) for more details